ATTRACTING YOUR KING & REIGNITING THE FLAME

BY MELISSA PORTIS

NEUROSCIENCE, PSYCHOLOGY, & FEMININE POWER

ISBN: 979-8-218-82312-2

Printed in United States of America

Cover Design: Melissa Portis

TABLE OF CONTENTS

INTRODUCTION

"Attracting Your King & Reigniting the Fire" Book Formula

Let's be honest, being in relationships can sometimes feel like you're wrestling with the devil. However, here's the thing: when you take a hard look at what's really going on beneath the surface, you start to understand yourself much better. It's like turning on a light in a dark room. Suddenly, you can see not just our own mess more clearly, but also what your partner might be going through. I'm telling you, facing the ugly truth ain't easy! Trust me, I know because I've been there. Having to unmask my mess gave me a reality check.

The more you work through your own baggage and learn to really listen and communicate, the stronger you'll become. That is the kind of self-awareness and emotional maturity that is incredibly attractive. It shows you're not just pretty on the outside; you're doing the real work on the inside to become someone who can build something meaningful and lasting with another person.

Before I met my king, I was already deep into the journey of self-improvement. My confidence was at its peak, built through persistent inner work and a commitment to crafting the life I envisioned. At that time, I was preparing to move to another state to go into ministry full time. I was ready to leave everything behind and start anew as a strong, high-value woman who knew she deserved the best. That's how I carried myself with purpose and poise.

The last piece of the puzzle was getting my body strong and in better shape. I knew I would be speaking to people in an impactful way. I wanted my physical presence to reflect how I felt inside. I wasn't in bad shape; it was the fact that I was pushing myself in every area of my life as much as I could. As I was traveling back and forth between states serving in a ministry, I had finally made the decision and joined a gym with my mother, offering her three different choices, and she chose one in the South Loop of Chicago.

We committed to going 3-4 times a week, and it became a beautiful bonding experience. As my waist slimmed and my body transformed, I felt more empowered than ever.

I was blessed with the best trainer in the gym (my partner), a master elite in fitness and bodybuilding who pushed both me and my mother to our limits. It was there, amidst the sweat and dedication, that I met my king, my destiny partner, my high-value man. Meeting him felt like the perfect culmination of all the work I had done on myself.

For years, I was fiercely independent. I handled car repairs, all the heavy lifting, college education for my kid, and even pumped my own gas! (Yes, I said it.) I thrived on self-reliance, making every decision on my own, a far cry from the support system I'd known growing up. But that independence, while empowering, also meant a certain solitude. I refused to settle for less than what I knew God had planned for me, patiently weeding through the "bad apples" until the golden one appeared.

Then, "boom!" My King arrived. But even then, my ingrained independence almost sabotaged everything. We'd have little "tug-of-wars" over mundane things like carrying cases of water, me stubbornly insisting, "I got it!" It was a battle between my ingrained self-sufficiency and his desire to provide. I finally realized that allowing him to be the man I'd prayed for was part of the divine plan. This is where the science of relationships truly kicked in. Our connection was instant and undeniable, relational magnetism, a powerful mix of chemistry, shared values, and, most importantly, reciprocity. God kept emphasizing this word, and I finally understood it wasn't just about me; it was about us two becoming one.

My King, who also happens to be my personal trainer and a wildly successful entrepreneur running two other businesses, perfectly articulated the concept: reciprocity is about emotional support, affection, mutual respect, and a balanced give-and-take.

He taught me so much about business skills, negotiation, and financial management. Together, we even run a wellness boutique called SnuggFitt! This financial security and business success dramatically increased my self-worth and value.

It wasn't just about looking good; it was about feeling valued and secure, the kind of woman who attracts a high-value man. I had to do the inner work on myself first before I could attract him. You have to start becoming what you want.

I also had to refine my communication style. I learned to speak with a softer tone, being that delicate flower, yet still getting my point across effortlessly. It's a superpower, let me tell you! And the most amazing thing? My quirks, the things I used to hide, became endearing. My partner loves my bizarre dreams! It was something I was embarrassed about because they are so out of this world. When I decided to share a dream with him, she was so elated that he actually shared with me that he interprets dreams.

We were two peas in a pod; we both smiled at each other. This is the power of authenticity. Let your true self shine! My past experiences had left me crippled by fear, but my King helped me break free. He instilled in me a fearless, bold woman. He would not have been able to do this if I weren't already on my own journey to freedom. It's like a baby the moment it enters the world, it simply trusts. It breathes, it cries, and it receives love without questioning if it deserves it. I overcame those fears quickly.

Attending business meetings, sales, recruiting, negotiations, some were smooth, some were rough, but I did them, transforming me into the woman I am today. Confident and self-assured. Remember the movie G.I. Jane? She overcame all odds, facing ridicule and adversity to become fearless. That's the kind of inner strength that makes you a high-value woman. I learned to live for myself, not for others' approval. This decision led to a much greater life. I took risks, ignoring those side-eyes, refusing to limit my opportunities because of others' opinions. I broke free from the limitations that others had placed on me. I did the inner work, and now I know my worth. Are relationships perfect? Absolutely not. But if you know you've met your King, don't waver, no matter what. Being with my partner made me more self-assured. It's like that push I needed, that fine tuning which, in turn, amplified my value as a woman.

Ladies, hear me well when I say this, master emotional intelligence. It's the secret weapon! I used to be an emotional rollercoaster. I still feel emotions deeply, but I've learned to control them. Handle business like a boss with logic and strategy, then go have a good cry in the car later. Emotional intelligence is the game, and I've become very good at it.

It starts with self-awareness. Recognize your insecurities and flaws and actively work on them. I knew I wanted to get fit, and I also knew my weaknesses. So, when someone criticized me, I didn't get emotional; I'd say, "Okay, tell me something I don't know." I handled it with confidence as a self-assured woman. I've learned to strategize, to anticipate others' moves in business. Being underestimated, especially in a male-dominated business world, is actually a gift. It allows me to control the situation. I let them talk, I let them underestimate me, because I'm playing chess, not checkers. I don't need to interrupt and let them know who I am. I educate myself *beforehand* to avoid being blindsided. I come armed with information and confidence. Learn the ability to understand and manage your emotions, and to understand and influence the emotions of others. If you master this, your value as a woman will skyrocket.

Let's take a look at some steps in detail that help put me in position to attract my King.

Get Your Bag Up: Achieve Financial Independence

First things first, I've always been independent, but I knew I had to step it up and create a life that was financially secure. I started budgeting like a boss and even took on a side hustle connecting with small businesses doing management and office work that turned my passion into profit. Not only did this increase me financially, but it also boosted my confidence, which is oh-so-attractive! Here's what I did:

- Set clear financial goals.
- Started saving and investing early.
- Explored side hustles that aligned with my interests.

When I met my destiny partner, my king, it felt like a divine alignment of our paths! Since I was already on the journey of financial independence, God introduced me to someone who could elevate my finances even further. Imagine this: my credit score was skyrocketing, credit card companies were lining up to offer me their best deals, and suddenly, I was receiving credit line increases that were beyond my wildest dreams!

But it didn't stop there. My partner saw potential in me that I hadn't fully realized. He invited me to co-own a fitness and wellness company, giving me the opportunity to learn the ins and outs of business and become a successful entrepreneur, not just an employee. It was all about understanding what it takes to build revenue and lead with confidence. This experience taught me that faith without works is dead. When you do the work and align yourself with your goals, God takes care of the rest.

Invest in Personal Development: Grow and Evolve

I believe that to attract the best, you must be the best version of yourself. I enrolled in workshops, read books, and even coaching and mentorship. It was all about growing spiritually, emotionally, and intellectually. This growth not only made me feel more fulfilled but also made me a more interesting and engaging person. ***Here's how you can start:***

- Identify areas where you want to grow.
- Seek out resources like books, courses, or mentors.

- Set personal development goals and track your progress.

Since I was already deep into my self-development journey, preparing myself for the amazing things God had in store, meeting my king was like the universe saying, "You're ready!" He introduced me to some life-changing books that shifted my perspective on why we experience certain challenges. One standout was "Outwitting the Devil," which opened my eyes to the hidden battles we face.

Another gamechanger was "Think and Grow Rich," and "Atomic Habits" are must-reads for anyone looking to align their life with abundance and purpose. These books were like keys unlocking new levels of understanding and growth.

The universe has a way of aligning you with your God-given purpose and the person you're meant to be with in life. I hope you're catching the patterns here: it's all about alignment!

Communicate with Charisma: Engage with Warmth and Charm.

It was my charisma and warmth that caught my king's

attention. I learned to engage genuinely, listen actively, and speak from the heart. This doesn't mean being someone you're not but rather letting your authentic self-shine through.

Try these tips:

- Practice active listening shows genuine interest in others.
- Use positive body language and eye contact.
- Speak with empathy and kindness.

I was on a mission to enhance who I was as a woman. Being involved in ministry as a leader taught me the importance of communicating effectively. I learned that being an authentic listener builds trust far better than talking over people or pushing my opinions onto people.

He saw my genuine heart behind my efforts and recognized that I just needed a little polishing. Inviting me into his world, he demonstrated how to build lasting relationships with clients who became friends, and friends who turned into key players in growing the business.

Through his influence, I became authentically charming, discovering the power of genuine connections. He consistently built me up and poured into my growth. This approach brought out a warmth within me that radiated.

Let Your Laughter Reveal Your Softness

Laughter is such a powerful connector. I made it a point to let my humor and joy shine in conversations. It breaks down walls and shows your softer side, making interactions light and enjoyable. Here's how to let your laughter lead:

- Find joy in everyday moments.
- Share funny stories and jokes.
- Don’t be afraid to be silly sometimes!

This is an incredible way we connect on another level. One thing my destiny partner noticed about me early on was my playful, silly side. Anytime he felt uptight, I had this knack for lighting up the situation with humor. Even when I got nervous or needed to break the ice, I’d crack a joke to lighten the mood.

We laugh about anything, sharing jokes and smiles naturally. Sometimes it’s needed just to ease tension.

It’s like a catalyst that helped build a solid foundation of friendship that blossomed into a beautiful love story. Laughter became our secret language, strengthening our bond and keeping our relationship vibrant and joyful.

Ultimately, I had to make some hard decisions to surrender and connect to my husband. I had to let some people go and certain ideologies that would have kept me from fulfilling my purpose on this earth. I was being prepared and guided to the right person, my king at the right time.

My story is a testament that you can be a modern, independent woman and still have a heart full of faith without being "holier than thou." You can truly be yourself, enjoying the life that was created for you, and still attract a high-value man, a man of God to love you.

It's all about alignment. I’m keeping it real with you, let’s not always be quick to blame the devil for delays or for things that aren't going the way you want them to go. What you align with is what God, the universe will bring to you.

It’s up to you to choose much like the movie Matrix, choosing between the red pill or the blue pill. The length of your journey depends on how long it takes for you to surrender. Do the necessary work for yourself first and your king, your destiny partner, will meet you by divine appointment.

This isn't just my story; the good news is that I have a proven formula that I'm going to share with you!

UNMASKING THE "DEVIL"

Welcome to a transformative chapter of "Attracting Your King," where we're diving into the brave world of owning your ugly truth. Yep, it's time to get real about those relationship patterns that keep showing it's ugly head. But don't worry we're doing this with love, laughter, and a whole lot of grace. Let's get started!

Own Your Ugly Truth: Evaluate Relationship Patterns Without Shame

Let's be honest for a second. We all have those moments where our past relationships resemble a rollercoaster ride thrilling but sometimes a bit too wild! Food for thought oxytocin, dopamine, and serotonin are the hormones of bonding, pleasure, and security. These are key players in attraction. By cultivating self-awareness and emotional intelligence, you'll naturally draw in a partner who values authenticity and connection. It's time to take a good look at those patterns and evaluate them without a hint of shame. Why? Because recognizing these patterns is your first step toward transformation and growth.

Reflect Without Regret: Grab that journal and start jotting down the timelines of your past relationships.

What patterns do you see?

Impact Moves: Journal on past patterns with the lens of *learning*, not blame: *"What was I craving? What was I avoiding?"* **Use affirming language:** *"That version of me was doing her best. I know more now."*

Let go of "what-ifs" and replace them with "what's next."

Master This; The **"3L Reflection Model"**

- Look back kindly
- Learn something true
- Lead forward

This mindset keeps you emotionally available and not stuck in regret of loops that repel connection.

Ask the Tough Questions: What role did you play in these cycles?

Impact Moves:

Ask open-ended questions like:

- "What's something that shaped how you love?"
- "What does emotional safety look like to you?"
- Share your truth first, then invite him: *"I've learned to value emotional presence, what about you?"*

Avoid surface-level Q&A and go for soulful storytelling.

Master This; The **"Mirror & Deepen"** technique:

- Mirror his answer
- Add her insight
- Deepen the convo with curiosity

High-value men crave conversations that make them feel more like themselves...

Practice Kindness: This isn't about being harsh on yourself. It's about understanding and growing from your experiences.

Impact Moves

Acknowledge his efforts, even the small ones: *"Thank you for taking the time. That means a lot."*

- Replace criticism with curiosity or redirection.
- Give compliments that highlight *who he is*, not just what he does.

Master This; The **"Kindness Drop"** rule:

- Offer one sincere, specific kindness every time you connect verbal or nonverbal.
- Kindness is magnetic especially when it comes from strength, not performance.

Embrace Growth: By uncovering these patterns, you lay the groundwork for change.

Impact Moves

Share where she's working on herself: *"I'm learning to stay open even when things feel uncertain."*

- Ask what he's learning too; create growth-focused dialogue.
- Frame "mistakes" as lessons, not failures.

Master This; The **"Growth Check-In"**

Once a week, reflect: “What did I learn about myself, about him, and about how I love?”

Being in growth is more attractive than acting as if I have it all figured out. It keeps me radiant, real, and evolving.

No More Drama: Cultivate Emotional Intelligence

Drama might make for an entertaining TV series, but let’s be real, it's not something we want in our everyday lives. Cultivating emotional intelligence is about understanding your emotions and learning to manage them with grace and maturity. Emotional intelligence is the #1 predictor of relationship success, according to extensive research by Dr. John Gottman and Daniel Goleman.

High EQ reduces reactivity, increases empathy, and builds trust which are essential for attracting and maintaining a healthy relationship. Recognizing those moments when you feel a storm brewing inside and knowing how to navigate through it without causing a blow out in your relationship is crucial. Proverbs 16:32 reminds us, "Better a patient person than a warrior, one with self-control than one who takes a city." Start by identifying your triggers, the things that set you off and work on managing them with mindfulness.

Mind Your Triggers: Start identifying what sets you off and work on managing those triggers with mindfulness.

Impact Moves

- Identify her top 2–3 emotional triggers in relationships (e.g. silence = rejection).
- **Pause when triggered and name the emotion:** *"I feel dismissed. Not necessarily because of him, but because of past pain."*
- **Regulate before responding then decide:** *"Do I need clarity, or is this an old story?"*

Master This; The **"Name, Breathe, Reframe"** strategy:

1. *Name* the trigger
2. *Breathe* into the body
3. *Reframe* the story before engaging

Men are drawn to women who don't explode but also don't suppress. That's emotional grace.

Communicate with Empathy: Express your feelings clearly and listen actively. Emotional maturity is not just attractive, it's essential.

Impact Moves

Start with feelings, not accusations: *"I felt unheard earlier, and I want to feel close to you."*

- Mirror what he says to show understanding before sharing her own view.
- Soften your truth with sincerity: *"I'm not saying this to criticize, I just want us to feel more connected."*

Master This; The **"Feel Need Invite"** formula**:**

1. *"I feel..."*
2. *"I need..."*
3. *"Can we talk about that?"*

Empathy is not weakness. It's emotional elegance and highly magnetic.

Practice Mindfulness: Take deep breaths before responding and reflect on your feelings.

Impact Moves

Take a breath and ground yourself before responding in emotionally charged moments.

- **Stay curious:** *"What am I really feeling beneath this irritation?"*
- Notice how your tone, body, and presence impact the emotional quality of the moment.

Master This; Use the **"3-Second Softening Rule"**

When emotions spike, pause for 3 seconds before speaking.

1. Soften the voice.
2. Loosen the shoulders.
3. Speak with intention.

That calm presence? It's irresistible to secure, emotionally intelligent men.

Handle with Grace: Emotional intelligence allows you to handle conflicts calmly and maturely.

Impact Moves

Stay grounded in conflict; don't match his intensity, model emotional leadership.

- **Use soft starters:** *"I know this is a tender subject, but I want to understand your view..."*
- **Normalize repair:** *"I didn't love how that went; can we try again with more presence?"*

Master This; The **"Queen's Response Code"**

1. Stay calm
2. Stay kind
3. Stay clear

Grace under pressure makes you unforgettable and proves you're ready for a king, not a project.

Date Your Damn Self: Embrace Joyful Independence

Before you can attract your king, you need to be the queen of your own life. Embracing joyful independence is all about learning to love your own company and finding fulfillment within yourself. It's about realizing that you don't need someone else to complete you, you're already whole. Dedicate one night a week just for you. This is your time to indulge in whatever makes your heart sing. Cook your favorite meal, lose yourself in a good book, or dive into a hobby you've always wanted to try.

Solo Adventures: Dedicate one night a week just for you. Cook your favorite meal, indulge in a hobby, or simply unwind with a good book.

Impact Moves

Designate one "solo date night" weekly: Cook for yourself, try a new class, or explore a creative outlet.

- **Practice having fun and enjoying time by yourself:** *"I love that I can enjoy my own company, it's grounding and energizing."*
- Speak about your passions with enthusiasm. High-value men are drawn to women who *already feel alive.*

Master This; Use the **"Self-Sourcing Energy"** formula:

Pleasure + Presence + Purpose = Magnetic Energy.

The woman who enjoys herself is a woman worth pursuing.

Celebrate Yourself: Joyful independence is magnetic. A king wants a whole queen, not someone looking for their other half.

Impact Moves

Speak affirmingly about your life: *"I'm proud of how I handled this week. I really showed up for myself."*

- Gently correct self-deprecating humor, it erodes subconscious confidence.
- **Share wins and joys with warmth, not arrogance:** *"This brought me so much joy that I had to celebrate it."*

Master This; The **"Internal Applause Technique"**

Every day, acknowledge one thing you did well *without* needing external praise. A king doesn't crown a queen. She crowns herself and *he recognizes it.*

Adore yourself and let that energy carry you through the day.

Discover Passions: Joyful independence is magnetic and draws people to you.

Impact Moves

Explore 1–2 curiosity-driven interests without needing to monetize or perfect them.

- Pay attention to what lights you up in conversation, passions leave a trace of glow.
- **Share your interests confidently:** *"Lately, I've been obsessed with learning... it's bringing me back to life!"*

Master This; The **"Passion = Polarity"** principle:

When a woman is lit up by her life, she naturally creates emotional polarity and intrigue.

Passion makes her unforgettable even before the first touch.

Set the Tone: Embrace your independence to build a respectful and admirable relationship.

Impact Moves

- **Set expectations early:** *"I value space and individuality; it keeps me feeling grounded and open."* Avoid over-accommodation or quick availability; set boundaries and allow yourself to show up as your best self.
- **Normalize mutual respect and autonomy as sexy:** *"I admire people who love deeply without losing themselves."*

Master This; The **"Tone-Setting Trifecta"** in early interactions:

1. Voice independence with warmth
2. Demonstrate emotional self-sufficiency
3. Invite connection, not dependency

Independence isn't a wall. It's a doorway to higher-level love.

Take the Mask Off: Embrace Your True Self

Authenticity is your superpower. Genuine men lean in. Performative ones drift. It's time to drop the masks and let your true self shine. When you stop hiding behind facades, you invite genuine connections and attract people who appreciate the real you. It's about being unapologetically you, with all your quirks and imperfections. Take a moment to identify where you might be hiding your true self. Are there parts of you that you've been keeping under wraps because you're afraid of what others might think?

Be Authentic: Identify where you're hiding your true self and start embracing the real you. According to social psychology authenticity (not perfection) is what high value men really want. When we "drop the mask," we give others permission to do the same.

Impact Moves

Identify where you're "shape shifting" to gain approval, and ask: *"Is this who I truly am?"*

- Use real stories and language; ditch the polished script.
- Say what you mean, even if it's stern: *"I'd rather be myself than to be liked."*

Master This; The **"Drop the Mask"** reflection before dates or conversations:

1. *Am I trying to impress, or connect?*
2. *Is this really me, or a filtered version?*
3. *How can I be more honest without apologizing for it?*

The woman who risks realness is the one who commands deep, lasting connection.

Surround Yourself with Positivity: Keep company with those who love and accept you as you are.

Impact Moves

Choose friends, mentors, and environments that reflect your highest self, not old patterns.

- Notice who expands your light and who dims it and adjust accordingly.
- Speak positively about yourself and others. It keeps you in a magnetic frequency.

Master This; Practice the **“Vibe Audit”** every month:

Who am I around when I feel most myself? Who am I around when I shrink?

Men mirror how you hold yourself. Positive people reinforce your radiance, and a high-value man *feels* that.

Shine Brightly: Authenticity is your superpower. Let your true self shine.

Impact Moves

Share your weird, wild, or wonderful interests: *“I’ve always loved [x]..it just lights me up.”*

- Allow playfulness and joy to come through without filtering.
- **Practice self-appreciation**: *“I genuinely care about..., it's just a core part of who I am, and I wouldn't have it any other way..”*

Master This; Use the **"Soul Signal"** method on dates:

Express one thing that brings you joy and one value you live by. Genuine light is unmistakable, and it doesn't compete. It invites.

Attract Genuine Connections: Embrace who you truly are and invite meaningful relationships into your life.

Speak about what you really want in love, without performance: *"I value depth, passion, and growth. I'm not here for surface level connections."*

- Release people pleasing in favor of self-truth.
- Be patient, real love requires real presence.

Master This; The **"Aligned Attraction Formula"**

Truth + Warmth + Boundaries = The Right Men Stay, The Wrong Ones Fade.

Attraction isn't just about looks, it's about how *safe and seen* someone feels in your presence.

✨🩶✨ Melissa's Personal Tip To Make Your King Melt ✨🩶✨

Create safety for his shadow.

Say, "You don't have to be perfect babe because you're already perfect for me. I love you, flaws and all".

Men soften deeply when they feel emotionally safe to be imperfect.

You do this, they'll feel more comfortable letting their guards down.

CHAPTER Two

SHEDDING THE SKIN OF BLAME

Welcome to Chapter 2, where we're going to shed the skin of blame and embrace a life filled with confidence, understanding, and positivity. This chapter is all about transforming from within and creating the space for deeper, more meaningful connections. Ready to dive in? Let's go!

Confidence: Cultivate Self-Awareness and Responsibility

Confidence isn't just about strutting your stuff; it's rooted in self-awareness and taking responsibility for your actions. When you do this, you're actually firing up a crucial part of your brain, the prefrontal cortex.

This is where all our big decisions, future planning, and self-control happen. It's fascinating how simply owning up to our actions, instead of pointing fingers at others, can make such a difference in how we view ourselves and handle life's challenges.

When you understand yourself deeply, you can stand tall in your decisions and own your choices without deflecting blame. This isn't about beating yourself up for past mistakes, but rather about learning and growing from them. Take a moment to reflect.

Think about it: when we accept responsibility for our choices, we start believing more in our ability to shape our own destiny. This mindset tends to make us more confident, better at bouncing back from setbacks, and more skilled at building strong relationships with others. It's like a positive domino effect.

Start by reflecting on situations where you might have shifted blame onto others. What role did you play, and how can you take responsibility for your part?

Cultivating self-awareness is like building muscle the more you do it, the stronger and more confident you become.

Reflect on Your Role: Take time to understand your actions and their impacts.

Impact Moves

Ask yourself after interactions: *"How might my words or tone have sounded for him?"*

- **Use reflective language in conversations:** *"I realize I might have come across guarded; I want to be more open with you."*
- Notice habitual patterns (e.g., withdrawal, criticism) and pause before reacting.

Master This; Use the **"Impact Scan"** method. After every meaningful interaction, reflect on 3 questions:

1. What energy did I bring into the space?
2. What did I communicate nonverbally?
3. Did I invite closeness or create distance?

Own Your Choices: Accept responsibility for your decisions and learn from them.

Impact Moves: Use "I" statements over "you" blame

"I chose to stay silent when I needed to speak up that's on me."

- **Frame lessons, not failures:** *"That decision taught me a lot about what I value now."*
- Model emotional maturity by recognizing her triggers and responding, not reacting.

Master This; Use the **"Power Reframe"** method:

Instead of "He made me feel…," say "I felt ___, and I chose to ___."

This language quietly signals maturity and draws in men who respect self-aware leadership.

Build Self-Awareness: Regularly engage in self-reflection to strengthen your confidence.

Impact Moves

Take 5 minutes daily to journal: *"What did I learn about myself today?"*

- Tune into body cues during conversations such as: tight chest, racing thoughts, relaxed shoulders all give insight into inner emotional truth.
- Ask for feedback from trusted people: "What energy do I bring into a room?"

Master This; Use the **"Mirror Method"** before dates:

Ask,

1. Who is (your name) .....
2. What energy do I want to radiate?

3. What do I need to feel safe *and* open?

That inner alignment makes outer confidence magnetic.

Emotional Intelligence: Develop Empathy and Understanding

Emotional intelligence is your secret weapon for fostering deeper connections. It's about developing empathy and understanding for yourself and others, which creates a foundation of trust and respect. Start by putting yourself in others' shoes. How do they feel, and why might they be reacting a certain way? Practicing empathy allows you to respond with compassion rather than judgment. Developing this skill not only enhances your relationships but also enriches your life experience by opening your heart to the world around you.

Research in neuroscience shows that empathy activates brain regions like the anterior insula and anterior cingulate cortex, which are linked to regulating emotions and social understanding. From an attachment theory perspective, people with secure emotional patterns are more likely to express empathy and regulate their emotions, leading to healthier, more resilient romantic bonds. By combining insights from neuroscience, behavioral psychology, and communication science, you'll not only attract your king but to do so with clarity, emotional depth, and feminine power.

Practice Empathy: Regularly put yourself in others' shoes to understand their perspectives.

Impact Moves

Pause before responding and ask herself: *"What might he be feeling right now beneath his words?"*

- Reflect back on his emotions, not just his facts: *"It sounds like that really frustrated you."*
- Stay present instead of planning what to say, eye contact, head nods, and silence signal empathy.

Master This; Teach her to use the **"3 Levels of Listening"**

- What is he *saying*?
- What is he *feeling*?
- What does he *need*?

Respond with Compassion: Approach interactions with kindness and understanding.

Impact Moves

Use grounding touch or tone when emotions rise: A gentle hand or calm voice changes the entire dynamic.

- **Say:** *"That sounds horrible. I'm here for you hun."* instead of rushing to advice or judgment.
- **Normalize emotional expression:** *"It's okay to feel that way and I value your honesty."*

Master This; Use the **"Soften + Stay"** technique in conflict:

Soften voice, relax body, and stay emotionally present instead of pulling away or escalating.

This makes you emotionally irresistible and trustworthy.

Enhance Relationships: Use emotional intelligence to build trust and respect.

Impact Moves: Lead with curiosity, not assumption

"What did you mean by that?" opens connection.

- **Celebrate small emotional bids:** Respond when he shares; no matter how subtle.
- **Use "connection over correction":** Focus on maintaining warmth, even when disagreeing.

Master This; Use this to anchor every conversation in the **"TRU Formula"**

- **T**rust: Is my tone creating safety?
- **R**espect: Am I honoring his experience, even if I disagree?
- **U**nderstanding: Am I seeking to know, not just to be right or be nosey?

High-value men bond with women who lead with *emotional leadership,* not control.

Positive Energy: Replace Negativity with Positivity

Let's talk about energy specifically, the kind you radiate. Positive energy attracts positivity, while negativity can weigh you down. It's time to replace those negative thoughts and vibes with uplifting, empowering ones. Start by being mindful of your internal dialogue. When you catch yourself in a negative thought spiral, pause and reframe it with positivity. Surround yourself with positive influences, whether it's people, music, or activities that uplift your spirit. This shift not only transforms your outlook but also magnetizes positive experiences and people into your life. You know how people talk about "good vibes" and "bad vibes"? There's actually something fascinating behind that feeling we get from others.

When you're genuinely happy and confident, it shows not just in your smile, but in tiny signals you're probably not even aware of. Your body language shifts, your voice carries differently, and people pick up on that energy whether they realize it or not. Studies on emotional contagion, which is a spontaneous spread of emotions and related behaviors that can happen from one person to another shows that in a nutshell, positivity is contagious. Our brains are wired to connect with others who help us feel safe and uplifted.

Monitor Your Thoughts: Be aware of your internal dialogue and shift to positive thinking.

Impact Moves

Notice internal scripts like: *"I'm too much,"* or *"He's probably not into me."* Pause and reframe.

- **Replace doubt with grounded affirmations:** *"I bring value, warmth, and depth. Anyone would be lucky to be with me."*
- **Set an intention before connecting:** *"How do I want him to feel in my presence?"*

Master This; Use the **"Inner Talk Check-In"** before a date or conversation:

"Are my thoughts preparing me for connection or protection?"

Because attraction starts in the mind, not the mirror.

Surround Yourself Positively: Choose influences that uplift and inspire you.

Impact Moves

Curate a digital and social environment: Follow love-affirming content, not drama-driven media.

- Choose people who reflect the energy you want in a partner. Respect, emotionally present, purpose-driven…
- Protect your peace, "guard your heart for everything you do flows through it." Proverbs 4:23. Don't emotionally rehearse with those who drain you.

Master This; Apply the **"Emotional Mirror Rule"**

"What I consume, I become."

Ask yourself weekly: *Is this raising or lowering my standard for love?*

Attract Positivity: By radiating positive energy, you draw positive experiences and people.

Impact Moves

Enter conversations with emotional generosity: *"I'm excited to get to know you. I'm looking forward to..."*

- Use uplifting micro-expressions, smiles, open posture, and gentle laughter to signal warmth and safety.
- **Speak in future-positive language:** *"I love the idea of growing with someone. I believe the best relationships keep evolving."*

Master This; Learn the **"Radiance Reset"** technique before social interactions:

Think of 3 things you're grateful for → Smile gently → **Set the vibe:** "I'm here to *give* connection, not get approval." That shift in energy. It's pure magnetism.

Stronger Connections: Foster Communication and Trust

Building stronger connections requires open communication and trust. These are the pillars of any meaningful relationship, whether romantic or platonic.

Start by being open and honest in your interactions, expressing your feelings clearly and respectfully. Listen actively, showing genuine interest in others' perspectives. Trust is built over time through consistent actions and reliability. By fostering open communication and trust, you create a safe space where connections can flourish and deepen. Our brains contain special neurons called mirror neurons that activate both when we perform an action and when we observe someone else performing it. This phenomenon allows us to subtly align with another person, be it a partner or someone new we've met through body language, tone, and energy levels, fostering subconscious trust and emotional connection without any need for acting or pretending. Be genuine and real. Remember, "like attracts like". It's as if we have an internal mirror that helps us tune into the emotions and body language of others.

This is why, when you are with someone you truly trust, you might find yourself unconsciously mirroring their gestures or even finishing their sentences. Your brain is essentially syncing up with theirs, creating a deeper connection.

Communicate Openly: Express your feelings clearly and listen actively.

Impact Moves

Express feelings using "I feel + because + I need…" structure. Example:

- "I feel disconnected when I don't hear from you; I need reassurance that we're still aligned."
- Listen without interrupting or planning a response. Mirror his words before offering your take.
- **Replace passive hints with warm, direct truths:** *"Can I share something personal with you?"*

Master This; Use the **"Clear-Connect-Confirm"** method in conversations:

- **Clear** message
- **Connect** emotionally
- **Confirm** understanding

Open communication creates open hearts.

Build Trust: Consistent actions and reliability strengthen trust over time.

Impact Moves

Match your words with actions. If you say you value honesty, model it daily.

- **Communicate your standards without ultimatums:** *"Consistency is sexy to me, it builds trust."*
- **Give praise when he shows up well:** *"I really admire how grounded and consistent you are, it means a lot to me."*

Master This; Learn the **"Trust Stack"** model:

- **Say it**
- **Do it**
- **Repeat it**

Men trust women who are calm, clear, and congruent.

That's magnetic.

Create Safe Spaces: Foster an environment where open communication is welcomed.

Impact Moves

Create emotional safety through the "tone and timing" approach. This helps create a safe space where you both feel comfortable opening up and working through challenging conversations.

- **Use validating phrases:** *"That makes sense…"* or *"I get why you'd feel that way."*
- Respect his silence or processing time, it doesn't always mean disinterest.

Master This; Use the **"Anchor & Invite"** method in emotional moments:

Anchor: "We're okay, I love that we can talk about this."

Invite: "How are you feeling about it now?"

Safety is sexy. When a man feels emotionally safe, *he opens and stays*.

 Melissa’s Personal Tip To Make Your King Melt ✨🩶✨

Lead with ownership, not accusation.

Instead of saying, “You made me feel…” try,

“Babe, you mean the world to me. I caught myself, right before I was about to get out of my body. It's an old habit I'm trying to break. I really want to keep being open and real with you even if it’s difficult”.

Feeling stuck? *If you're reading this and thinking, "I have no idea how to move forward," don't worry! We've got your back. Visit* **MelissaPortis.com** *to request personalized support. Complete the short form under “Questions,” and we'll reach out to help you get unstuck and get you back on track. Do that now and come right back to the book.*

CHAPTER Three

THE UNBURDENING

Welcome to Chapter 3, where we're going to dive into letting go of all that emotional baggage weighing us down. It's time to shed what doesn't serve us anymore and step into a lighter, brighter version of ourselves. Ready to get real and set yourself free? Let's jump in!

Emotional Freedom: Release Resentment

Alright, let's cut to the chase. Resentment is like someone making you carry around a hideous looking bag that you don't even like. It's time to drop that baggage, ladies! Look at it this way, suppressed resentment and emotional rollercoasters activate the amygdala, which is an area of your brain responsible for processing emotions. Emotional acknowledgment is the key, not suppression. Emotional freedom means saying goodbye to the grudges and hello to a fresh start.

Start by taking a good, honest look at what you're holding onto. Is it really worth your energy? Spoiler: it's not. When you're free from emotional baggage, you exude positivity and openness. A high value man, a king is drawn to a woman who radiates peace and has room in her life for new possibilities.

Face It Head-On: Recognize those grudges and admit they're not helping you.

Impact Moves

Journal on any lingering resentment or unfinished emotional stories with questions like: "What am I still holding on to and why?"

- "Is this anger protecting something I'm afraid to feel?"
- **Say the truth aloud (to self or trusted coach/friend):** *"I haven't let this go because it made me feel powerless."*
- Acknowledge that holding on is costing your peace and presence.

Master This; The **"Truth Mirror Exercise"**

Look in the mirror and name what you're still holding onto without judgment. *"I'm still hurt by ___. But I'm choosing to free myself now."*

This clears energetic space to welcome someone emotionally present.

Let It Go: Decide to release it, even if you have to fake it till you make it.

Impact Moves

Start with *willingness*, even if you're not fully there: *"I'm open to not letting this define me anymore."*

- Write a "release letter" that you don't send, just to shift emotional charge.
- **Reframe:** *"That pain shaped me, but it doesn't get to have power over me."*

Master This; The **"Forgiveness Ladder"**

- Awareness
- Willingness
- Compassion
- Release

You don't have to feel ready; you just have to start climbing. Freedom creates space for *fresh, aligned love.*

Welcome the Good Stuff: Open up to positivity and new experiences.

Impact Moves

Start each day to simply receive. It's a way of showing up for the day with open arms instead of clenched fists.

- "What am I allowing in today?"
- Say *yes* to compliments without deflecting. Let yourself be seen, appreciated, celebrated.
- **Visualize emotional safety in love:** *"I welcome deep connection, truth, and peace."*

Master This; The **"3-Minute Receiving Exercise"** daily:

1. Place hand on heart
2. Breathe in gratitude
3. **Say:** *"I am open to receiving love and joy."*

Being open is magnetic because it signals, you're ready for *more*.

Inner Strength: Highlight Resilience and Empathy

Inner strength isn't just about powering through it's about bouncing back and being kind along the way.

Resilience is not fixed, it's trainable. According to neuroscience, when we bounce back, we strengthen neural circuits linked to adaptability, self-trust, and optimism which are core traits of emotionally mature, magnetic women. Resilience is your ticket to handling whatever life throws at you, and empathy is the secret sauce that makes you relatable and grounded. When things get tough, lean into your resilience. And don't forget empathy. It helps you connect and understand others, making you a high value woman in your relationship. Together, they're your dynamic duo for living life like the queen you are.

Flex Your Resilience Muscle: Keep bouncing back, stronger each time.

Impact Moves

- **Reframe setbacks:** *"This didn't break me, it built me."*

- **Celebrate bounce-backs, not just wins:** *"I didn't quit. I kept showing up."*
- **Ask empowering questions:** *"What did this teach me about what I deserve in love?"*

Master This; Use the **"3 R's of Resilience"**

- **Recognize** the trigger
- **Reframe** the meaning
- **Reset** with aligned action

High-value men respect women who rise with grace.

Empathy Wins: Put yourself in others' shoes and build deeper connections.

Impact Moves

Listen to understand, not to fix or defend: *"What might he be feeling underneath that?"*

- Mirror emotional energy before offering your perspective.
- **Replace assumptions with curiosity:** *"Help me understand, what's this like for you?"*

Master This; The **"Pause & Presence"** technique in conflict:

- Pause before reacting
- Get curious
- Reflect his emotional truth before adding your own.

Empathy doesn't mean losing your truth, it means opening the door to *him.*

Rock Life's Challenges: Use both resilience and empathy to handle life with grace.

Impact Moves

Navigate tough conversations with both honesty and warmth.

- Show strength without defensiveness, and softness without self-abandonment.
- **Model emotional maturity:** *"I can hold space for both of us, even when it's hard."*

Master This; The **"Soft & Spine Strategy"**

Strong spine (clear values + boundaries). Soft front (open heart + presence).

This is the kind of emotional elegance that magnetizes a man who's *ready*, not just available.

Forgiveness and Peace: Embrace Peace and Harmony

Forgiveness isn't about letting someone off the hook, it's about freeing yourself from the past. It's not about them; it's about your peace of mind. When you forgive, you open the door to living a more peaceful, harmonious life. And who doesn't want that?

Seriously, holding onto grudges is like drinking expired milk, it makes you sick. Start with forgiving yourself and realize everyone makes mistakes. Then, extend that forgiveness to others. A king is drawn to a partner who has let go of past baggage and is open to building a future together. When you embrace forgiveness, you clear the path for genuine connection and love. Start with You! Forgive yourself first and foremost.

Let Go of the Past: Release others from your mental grip and find peace.

Impact Moves

Acknowledge the mental grip: *"What story am I still living from?"*

- Genuinely forgive someone that you've been holding a grudge against. This frees you energetically.
- **Practice choosing peace over replay:** *"This doesn't define me anymore."*

Unprocessed emotional memories stay "alive" in the nervous system. When we replay old wounds, we unconsciously filter the present through the past. Letting go clears neural space for connection, joy, and new attraction patterns.

Master This; The **"Name & Neutralize"** method:

Name the old wound or pattern: *"I've been holding onto betrayal."*

- **Say:** *"That was then. This is now."*
- Take one aligned action toward your new standard in love.

Letting go isn't about erasing, it's about *elevating.*

Live in Harmony: Allow forgiveness to set you free and bring tranquility.

Impact Moves

Forgive *for yourself*, not the other person: *"I deserve freedom more than I need closure."*

- Choose forgiveness as an act of power, not permission.
- Replace "why did this happen to me?" with "what is this here to teach me?"

Master This; The **"HOPE Loop"** for inner harmony:

1. **Honor** the hurt
2. **Own** your power to heal
3. **Practice** emotional release
4. **Evolve** your story into wisdom

Forgiveness isn't weak, it's the gateway to *wholeness*. And wholeness is very attractive.

🩶 Melissa's Personal Tip To Make Your King Melt 🩶

Reveal your emotions without overdoing it.

Try saying,

"Sometimes I feel like I have to hold it all together hun, but I'm learning to let myself be vulnerable. Thank you for giving me that space, with you, to do so".

This creates intimacy through vulnerability, not pressure.

CHAPTER

Four

TAMING THE DEVIL

Welcome to Chapter 4, where we're focusing on taming those inner devils that can wreak havoc in our lives.

This chapter is about setting boundaries, fostering honest connections, and finding emotional stability. Ready to dive in and see how this can also help attract your king? Let's get started!

Self-Respect: Establish Boundaries

Let's talk about self-respect. Establishing boundaries isn't just a power move, it's a necessity. Boundaries protect your peace and show others how you expect to be treated. When you stand firm in your self-respect, you create an environment where only those who respect you can enter. This self-assuredness is magnetic. A king is drawn to a queen who knows her worth and isn't afraid to demand the respect she deserves.

Know Your Worth: Understand your value and set boundaries that reflect it.

Impact Moves

Ask: *"What is the version of me that no longer tolerates X?"*

- List 3 values you want reflected in every relationship.
- **Practice impactful affirmations:** *"If I wouldn't do it to me, I won't accept it from him."*

Master This; The **"Mirror Worth"** before any date or tough conversation:

Look in the mirror, make eye contact with yourself, and say: "You are worthy of clarity, care, and consistency."

When you know your value, you don't chase it.

Communicate Clearly: Let others know your limits and enforce them consistently.

Impact Moves: Use "I" statements

"I need space when I'm overwhelmed not because I'm angry, but because I value calm."

- Stop over-explaining. Clarity is enough.
- Frame boundaries as standards for connection, not rules for control.

Master This; Teach the **"Boundary Bridge"** format:

Appreciation or truth *"I've enjoyed our time..."*

- **Boundary:** *"...and I need slower pacing to feel emotionally safe."*
- **Reconnect or redirect:** *"If that aligns, great if not, I understand."*

Direct doesn't mean harsh. Clear = to the point. Fuzzy = masking.

Protect Your Peace: Boundaries keep negativity out and positivity flowing.

Impact Moves

Use silence or distance when needed not as punishment, but as nervous system regulation.

- **Set digital boundaries:** No explaining emotions via text.

- Audit what drains you then choose to opt out *before* burnout.

When your boundaries are constantly crossed, it can increase stress and disrupt your nervous system, making genuine connections challenging. The polyvagal theory explains how this affects the autonomic nervous system making it chaotic. Establishing clear boundaries can reduce stress and enhance emotional balance, making you deeply more attractive.

Master This; The **"Peace Preservation Protocol"**

A 3-part checklist you'll run before saying yes: Does this support my nervous system?

1. Will I feel proud of this tomorrow?
2. Does it align with the kind of relationship I'm calling in?

Boundaries aren't barriers, they're filters for *higher-quality connections.*

Be Crystal Clear: Create Honest Connections

Honesty is the foundation of any strong relationship.

Being crystal clear in your communication fosters trust and transparency. When you create honest connections, you build a strong bond that can withstand challenges.

A king values authenticity and will be drawn to someone who communicates openly and honestly. By being clear about your needs and expectations, you invite a deeper, more meaningful connection.

Practice Transparency: Be open and honest in your communications.

Impact Moves

Start with small truths: "I'm nervous and excited right now. It feels good to share that."

- **Let him see your emotional world without performance:** *"I don't have it all figured out and I'm okay with that."*
- **Use direct-yet-kind statements like:** *"Here's where I'm at with this... what about you?"*

Master This; Teach the **"Real > Perfect"** rule:

If you're choosing between being liked and being known, being *known* wins hands down. Authenticity fast-tracks intimacy.

Express Your Needs: Clearly articulate your desires and expectations.

Impact Moves

Replace hints with directness: "I feel most connected when…"

- **Use "need language" over complaint language:** "I need more clarity," vs. "You're confusing."
- Get clear on *your* needs before expressing them to others.

Master This; The **"Feel Need Request"** formula**:**

"I feel **[fill in with an emotion]** because I need **[fill in with what you value].** Would you be open to **[fill with a specific request]?**" E.g., "I feel disconnected because I need emotional intimacy. Would you be open to dinner this week?"

Build Trust: Honest connections foster trust and strengthen bonds.

Impact Moves

Match words with actions (and choose men who do the same).

- Build trust incrementally, don't overshare before a foundation is present.
- **Reflect trust-building behaviors in him:** "I noticed how you followed up like you said that means a lot to me."

Master This; Use the **"Trust Triangle"** (from Harvard's Center for Public Leadership).

1. **Authenticity** – Show up real
2. **Logic** – Speak clearly & with consistency
3. **Empathy** – Make others feel seen

When all three are present, trust sticks. If one is missing, attraction may not last.

Emotional Stability: Find Peace Through Boundaries

When we face danger or feel uneasy about something, our bodies enter survival mode, triggering the fight or flight response. This floods the system with adrenaline and cortisol, causing heart pounding, rapid breathing, and muscle tension. This primal reaction prepares us to handle threats, whether it's a public speech or a looming deadline. While intense, it's our body's protective mechanism. That's why it's so important to be emotionally stable. It's like the calm in the storm. It's about finding peace through the boundaries you set.

When you're emotionally stable, you navigate life's ups and downs with grace. This stability is incredibly attractive, as it signals that you're someone who can handle life's challenges with confidence. A king is drawn to a partner who brings peace and stability into his life, not drama. Establishing emotional stability through boundaries allows you to maintain your peace and attract a relationship that thrives on harmony.

Find Your Center: Use boundaries to maintain emotional balance.

Impact Moves

Check in before reacting: *"Is this response coming from fear or clarity?"*

- Use breathwork or grounding before emotionally charged conversations.
- **Set energetic boundaries:** *"I'm responsible for my energy, not someone else's chaos."*

Master This; The **“3-Point Centering Check-In”** before you communicate:

- What am I feeling?
- What do I need right now?
- How do I want to show up in this moment?

From this place, you speak, not react. That’s magnetic.

Handle with Grace: Approach life’s challenges with calm and confidence.

Impact Moves

Practice “the pause” in conflict: *“I care about this, so I want to respond with clarity, not heat.”*

- **Use emotion-labeled language:** *“I feel disappointed, not because of ...., but because I value consistency.”*
- **Communicate boundaries *without drama*:** “That doesn’t work for me, but I respect your decision."

Master This; Use the **“Golden Gap Rule”**

Give yourself 3 seconds before replying in conflict. In that space, choose dignity.

Men remember grace under pressure; it signals deep feminine self-mastery.

Attract Harmony: Emotional stability invites a peaceful, loving relationship.

Impact Moves

Prioritize inner peace over being "right" or dominant.

- Use tone, pacing, and body language to convey warmth and calmness.
- Let silence be a part of emotional connection, don't rush to fill every pause or silent space.

Master This; The **"Emotional Invitation Technique"**

Instead of fixing or proving, ask: "How are you really doing with this?"

"Would it feel good to talk about this later when we're both grounded?"

This emotional grace creates intimacy without intensity.

✨🩶✨ Melissa's Personal Tip To Make Your King Melt ✨🩶✨

Respond with grace when you want to react with fire.

Use the power of the pause. Whisper instead of yell.

Say,

"Part of me wants to fight, but I love us too much to go there."

That calm in the storm. He won't be able to resist you.

Feeling stuck? *If you're reading this and thinking, "I have no idea how to move forward," don't worry! We've got your back. Visit* ***MelissaPortis.com*** *to request personalized support. Complete the short form under "Questions," and we'll reach out to help you get unstuck and get you back on track. Do that now and come right back to the book.*

EMBRACING YOUR GOD-GIVEN POWER

Welcome to Chapter 5, where we're going all in on embracing that amazing, God given power inside you.

It's time to get real, channel your inner royalty, and let your confidence shine like the queen you are. Ready to strut your stuff and own your throne? Let's dive in!

Discovering the Queen Within

There's a queen inside every single one of us, just waiting to break free. It's all about recognizing your unique strengths and letting them shine in the world.

According to strengths-based psychology, women who regularly acknowledge and express their strengths activate higher levels of confidence, self-esteem, and relational magnetism. This is a strong, often irresistible attraction between individuals, much like the pull between magnets. The brain associates self-assured language with leadership and trust. Think about queen Esther from the Bible, who embodied beauty, favor, grace, and intelligence (Esther 2:7-17). She was a true queen who knew her worth and embraced her purpose.

When you embrace who you truly are, you begin living your life with purpose and passion. No more playing small, you're here to stand out and win.

Spot Your Superpowers: Take a moment to recognize what makes you uniquely awesome. Like Esther, embrace the qualities that make you stand out.

Impact Moves

Name 3 non-physical superpowers (e.g., empathy, humor, vision).

- Share your strengths in stories, not statements. **For example:** "In hard moments, I usually bring calm to the people around me. That's something I value about myself."
- Use confident self-acknowledgement in dating without downplaying it.

Master This; The **"Power Profile Formula"** to express strength with softness:

"People tell me I'm really **[insert strength],** and I've come to see that's true, it's helped me in relationships and in how I show up for others." This signals humble confidence. It's like catnip for high-value connections.

Celebrate Your Uniqueness: Flaunt what makes you different, it's your secret sauce! Look at how Michelle and Barack Obama complement each other with charisma and intelligence, each shining in their own light.

Impact Moves

Share something "weird but wonderful" on early dates: *"I dance to 90s R&B every Saturday morning, it's my reset button."*

- Speak about what you value even if it's niche, men of substance respond to substance.
- Reference iconic examples of couples who thrive by being different but aligned (like the Obamas, or Oprah and Stedman).

Master This; The **"Spark Story Share"** in conversation:

"One thing that makes me light up is **[insert passion or interest].** It's kind of my thing, and I love that it's not for everyone." Uniqueness becomes a filter, not a flaw.

Own Your Path: Step boldly into your journey with all the confidence of a reigning queen. Think of Pauletta Washington, who stood by Denzel during tough times, embodying wisdom and self-control (Esther 4:14-17).

Impact Moves

Speak your path into existence: *"This season of my life is about building deeper emotional intimacy, and I'm being intentional about who I share that with."*

- Ground confidence in *quiet clarity*, not hustle energy.
- Use models like queen Esther from the bible or Pauletta Washington as affirmations of grace, timing, and divine alignment.

Master This; The **"Crown Walk Statement"**

"I'm not rushing anything, I'm choosing everything."

That one line can change the dynamic of any conversation. It signals self-worth, presence, and discernment all hallmarks of a woman who's already royalty.

When you own your journey and step into your power, you become unstoppable. Just like these powerful couples, your strength and grace can attract and sustain a meaningful partnership.

Confidence Is Magnetic: Carry Yourself with Poise

Confidence is like wearing your favorite pair of heels; it elevates everything! When you carry yourself with poise, you're telling the world you know your worth and you're not afraid to show it. Somatic psychology shows that posture and body language directly affect hormonal response. *Expansive posture increases testosterone (power) and decreases cortisol (stress).*

How a woman carries herself shifts how others perceive and respond to her within seconds. This kind of confidence is like a magnet, drawing people and opportunities to you. A king can't help but notice a queen who walks with grace and assurance.

Stand Tall: Use body language that screams confidence.

Impact Moves

Use the **“2-Minute Power Pose”** before dates or tough conversations (feet planted, chest lifted, shoulders relaxed).

- Avoid closed-off gestures like crossing arms, looking down, or hunching.
- Anchor herself in the room by standing or sitting with poise back straight, head lifted.

Master This; The **“Mirror Check-In”** daily:

“If I saw me walking into a room right now, would I trust her? Be inspired by her? Want to know her?”

Your presence speaks before your voice does, train it to say “queen”, “I’m “more than enough. Look in the mirror and say “wow, I’m an incredible woman”.

Create personalized affirmations on how you want to be seen.

Show It Off: Let your actions and words reflect how sure you are of yourself.

Impact Moves

Slow down your speech slightly, this signals grounded-ness and power.

- Replace filler words (like "just," "sorry," or "I think") with ownership language: *"I believe," "I want," "I've decided."*
- Speak with warmth *and* direction; blend feminine softness with confident clarity.

According to communication science, tone, pacing, and certainty in speech makes someone more persuasive and attractive than just what they say. Confidence in communication cues emotional intelligence and leadership.

Master This; The **"Queen's Voice"**

- Read a powerful quote aloud daily in a confident tone.
- Record and play back to hear how her energy lands.
- Adjust posture, breath, and tone to sound like her highest self.

Men don't fall for perfection; they respond to emotional certainty.

Attract Like a Magnet: Your confidence pulls in the right people and vibes.

Impact Moves

Let confidence be quiet, own your space without overexplaining or overperforming.

- Respond with calmness when others try to impress you, it shifts the dynamic from chasing to choosing.
- Use intentional pauses and eye contact to create intrigue and magnetism.

Master This; The **“Queen Energy Mantra”** before social settings:

“I don’t chase. I attract. I trust my presence speaks before I do.” Confidence isn’t about being loud; it’s about being *undeniable*.

Self-Worth Sets Standards: Set Boundaries and Attract Respect

Knowing your worth is your superpower, and it sets the stage for everything else. When you know your value, you naturally set boundaries that protect your peace and demand respect. This isn’t about being bossy, it's about respecting yourself enough to say, "This is what I deserve." A king respects a queen who knows her worth and stands by it.

Define Your Standards: Clearly outline what you value and expect.

Impact Moves

Write down your top 5 non-negotiables for partnership (e.g., emotional availability, kindness, spiritual alignment).

- **Practice *naming* your standards early with elegance:** "For me, connection looks like presence, consistency, and shared growth."
- Don't confuse "standards" with "preferences." One is non-negotiable. The other is flexible.

Master This; The **"3-Layer Standard Check"** to clarify what's truly essential:

- Is this about *values*, not ego?
- Does it support my *peace*, not just pleasure?
- Would I model this for my future children or friends?

Keep Those Boundaries Firm: Never waver on what protects your worth.

Impact Moves

Express boundaries with calm conviction: "That doesn't work for me. I honor your choice, but I won't participate in that dynamic."

- Avoid negotiating with guilt. Your worth isn't up for debate.
- Notice red flags early and respond, not explain.

Psychological boundary is a theory that confirms that clear, consistently enforced boundaries are essential for self-esteem and healthy relationships. People respect what is *defined and reinforced.*

Master This; The **"Soft No, Solid Yes"** framework**:**

"I care about our connection, but I need **[boundary].** If that's not aligned, I understand and I trust the right people will respect that." This blends compassion and clarity in the formula for feminine power.

Demand Respect: Your self-worth sets the tone for how others treat you.

Impact Moves

Use self-respecting body language: direct eye contact, slow movements, strong posture.

- **Normalize calling out disrespect kindly but firmly:** "I'm not okay with being spoken to that way. Let's take space if needed."
- Be willing to walk away. Confidence in boundaries creates a gravitational pull.

Social learning theory shows that we train others how to treat us by what we tolerate and how we reinforce behavior. Respect is often communicated nonverbally before it's spoken.

Master This; The **"Mirror Rule"** in dating:

"If someone treated you the way you treat yourself, would you stay?" If the answer is yes, you're already setting the tone for deep, mutual respect.

Radiance from Within: Shine with Inner Confidence

Now, your glow comes from within. Inner confidence is your light, and when you let it shine, it's irresistible. It's about being comfortable in your own skin and letting that energy light up your world. A king is drawn to a queen whose confidence radiates from within, inspiring everyone around her.

Cultivate Your Glow: Focus on growth and self-love to boost your inner confidence.

Impact Moves

Begin a daily “Glow Ritual” that centers joy and celebration (dance, music, journaling, prayer).

- Acknowledge daily wins, no matter how small this rewires the brain toward confidence.
- Speak affirmations out loud before dates or hard conversations to activate positive neural pathways.

Master This; The **“Inner Glow Formula”**

Self-love (practice) + Joy (permission) + Gratitude (presence) = Magnetic Confidence.

High-value men sense when a woman is lit from within, its emotional gold.

Let It Shine: Allow your confidence to light up your actions and interactions.

Impact Moves

Speak with passion and feeling: *"I absolutely love mornings, they feel like a fresh beginning to something great."*

- Let facial expressions reflect how you *feel*, not just what you *think*.
- Don't shrink when complimented, receive it with, *"Thank you, I receive that."*

Master This; The **"Open Energy Language"** method:

Swap dull phrases like "I'm fine" with *"I'm feeling grateful today, I feel aligned."* Men of depth are drawn to women who *feel deeply and show it without fear.*

Inspire Others: Your radiance encourages others to find their own light.

Impact Moves

Celebrate others openly. Confident women lift other people up, not compete.

- **Use joy as a leadership tool:** *"I really admire how you handled that. It inspired me."*
- **Share your story with others:** "I didn't always feel this way, learning to love myself changed everything."

Master This; The **"Radiant Ripple Rule"**

"When I shine, I give permission for others to do the same." This creates emotional safety, admiration, and connection, all signals of a woman who leads with love and self-worth.

 Melissa's Personal Tip To Make Your King Melt 

Own your desire out loud.

High-value men love a woman who knows what she wants without apology.

Say:

"I want to feel cherished, claimed, and wildly adored. When we're together and you look at me, I want to feel like I'm the only woman in the room".

RISE ABOVE THE SHADOWS

Welcome to Chapter 6, where we focus on rising above the shadows and embracing the strength that comes from within. This chapter is all about harnessing grace, finding peace amidst chaos, and turning life's challenges into steppingstones for wisdom. Ready to elevate your journey? Let's dive in!

Grace Over Reaction: Develop Self-Control

Life can be a wild ride, right? And sometimes, the urge to react impulsively is real. But here's the deal, true power lies in taking the high road with grace.

Developing self-control means hitting the pause button right before you react, giving you the chance to respond thoughtfully. Neuroscientific research shows that taking at least 6 seconds to pause activates the prefrontal cortex, calming emotional reactivity and increasing the ability to respond rationally and compassionately. This isn't about hiding your emotions but choosing how to express them like the queen you are. Practicing grace when things get tough not only boosts your confidence but also earns major respect. Someone who can keep their cool is nothing short of magnetic!

By mastering grace over reaction, you naturally attract a king who admires your ability to handle life's curveballs with poise. A partner who values stability will be drawn to your calm and collected demeanor, seeing you as a rock in stormy weather.

Pause and Reflect: Give yourself a sec to gather your thoughts before reacting.

Impact Moves

Take a silent breath or sip of water before responding to difficult or emotionally charged moments.

- **Create personal "pause phrases" like:** "Give me a second, I want to respond clearly." "I'm just taking that in for a moment."
- Recognize the bodily signals of reactivity; tight chest, quick breath, tension and pause when they show up.

Master This; Use the **"6-Second Reset Rule"**

Breathe in for 3, out for 3. This small shift disengages autopilot and empowers you to regain control.

Mindfulness Magic: Try some mindfulness exercises to boost your self-awareness.

Impact Moves

Begin your day with 3 minutes of body-scan meditation to tune into yourself.

- Use micro-mindfulness breaks before dates, texts, or difficult convos: *hand over heart, close eyes, one deep breath.*
- Practice naming your emotion silently before expressing it.

Master This; Teach the **"Feel > Name > Choose"** technique:

- Feel it (without judgment)
- Name it ("I'm feeling tense / hopeful / excited")
- Choose your next action from intention, not impulse.

Respond with Intention: Choose your words and actions wisely to reflect your inner strength.

Impact Moves

Frame communication with purpose: "My intention isn't to blame, it's to understand and share what matters to me."

- **Replace reactive language with grounding language:** "Here's what I'm feeling right now and what I need moving forward…"
- Practice "feminine clarity" warm, emotionally grounded truths without needing to defend them.

Master This; The **"Mirror Before Message"**

Ask: *"Would I feel safe, respected, and seen if someone spoke to me the way I'm about to speak to him?"*

This rewires your default from reaction to respectful resonance.

Stay Grounded in Chaos: Maintain Inner Peace

Research in cognitive appraisal theory shows that our emotional responses are based not just on events, but on how we *interpret* circumstances and events. Women who train themselves to reframe stressors create internal stability that others feel immediately. In a world that sometimes feels chaotic, staying grounded is your superpower. Keeping that inner peace amidst the chaos means finding your happy place whether it's meditating, praying, or just chilling. Inner peace isn't about avoiding chaos; it's about keeping your cool when the world's going nuts. Master this skill, and you'll be a beacon of tranquility, attracting those who appreciate your peaceful vibes and stability.

A king is naturally drawn to someone who exudes calm and serenity. Your ability to maintain inner peace signals that you're someone who can create a harmonious life together, a trait that's incredibly appealing for any potential partner.

Find Your Anchor: Discover what keeps you centered and calm.

Impact Moves

Develop an "anchor thought" to ground you in emotionally charged moments: "I don't need to control this; I just need to stay rooted in me."

- **Ask this reframe question when triggered:** "Is this happening *to* me or *for* me?"
- Use sensory cues (bracelet, essential oil, mantra) to snap out of spirals and back into center.

Master This; The **"Meaning Before Reaction"**

Before responding to a man's behavior, pause to ask: *"What meaning am I giving this, and is it true?"*

This creates a calm, emotionally intelligent communication pattern that men deeply respect.

Create Your Sanctuary: Make a space or routine that brings peace and chill vibes.

Impact Moves

Design your living space as a reflection of the love and connection your calling in.

- Include soothing textures (velvet, linen), warm lighting, and visual cues of empowerment (art, affirmations).

- Use color psychology intentionally; lavender and soft pinks are shown to reduce anxiety and promote receptivity.

Master This; The **"Emotional Design Ritual"**

Ask: *"Does this space calm my nervous system and invite connection, or does it reflect chaos?"*

Then adjust even small corners (desk, bathroom, car) to mirror who you truly are.

Cultivate Calmness: Regularly do things that relax and rejuvenate you.

Impact Moves

Before a date or conversation, visualize how you *want* to feel after, not just during.

- "I want to leave this feeling light, proud, and peaceful."
- Choose calming activities that build long-term well-being, not short-term highs (e.g., nature walk over wine binge).

Use emotional forecasting in love: *"Is this dynamic likely to bring me peace or confusion?"*

Master This; The **"Pre-Feel Strategy"**

Before saying yes to something (a text reply, a night out, a serious convo), ask: *"How will this likely make me feel afterward? Is that feeling aligned with who I'm becoming?"*

Turn Pain into Power: Transform Struggles into Wisdom

Every struggle is like a plot twist waiting to turn into something amazing. Turning pain into power is about using those tough experiences as fuel for growth and wisdom. Instead of letting setbacks drag you down, see them as chances to level up. This shift in perspective turns challenges into steppingstones toward becoming an even stronger, wiser version of yourself. When you transform your struggles into stories of resilience, you inspire others and attract those who appreciate your depth and strength.

The ability to turn pain into power is incredibly attractive to a king who seeks a partner of substance and character. Your resilience and wisdom show that you're someone who can face life's challenges head-on and come out stronger on the other side.

Reframe Challenges: See struggles as opportunities to learn and grow.

Impact Moves

Use empowering language when discussing setbacks: "That experience taught me..." instead of "I messed up again."

- Catch "fixed mindset" phrases like **"I always attract the wrong men" and reframe them:** "I now recognize patterns and I'm making better choices."
- Speak of your past from the lens of a woman who *overcame*, not one who *was defined by pain.*

Master This; The **"Rewrite It to Rise"** practice:

Pick one disempowering belief and rewrite it as a lesson or turning point. Ex: "He abandoned me" → "That moment reminded me of the love and respect that I truly deserve."

Learn and Evolve: Take lessons from painful experiences to build your wisdom bank.

Impact Moves

Reflect regularly on key moments in her love life: "What did I believe then? What do I believe now?"

- **Identify emotional upgrades:** "Old me would've chased. New me breathes and lets go."
- Tell your story as an evolution, not a victim loop.

Master This; The **"Then vs. Now"** exercise:

Write two journal entries: "What I thought love was…"

"What I now know love is…"

This builds the emotional narrative of a woman who knows herself.

Inspire Others: Share your journey and empower those around you.

Romans 5:3-4 reminds us, "We also glory in our sufferings, because we know that suffering produces perseverance; perseverance, character; and character, hope." This scripture underscores the transformative power of overcoming challenges.

Melissa's Personal Tip To Make Your King Melt

Speak life into him.

Say this,

"I feel so protected when I'm with you. Just you being here with me makes me feel so secure".

Affirm his energy, and you'll watch him rise into it.

Feeling stuck? *If you're reading this and thinking, "I have no idea how to move forward," don't worry! We've got your back. Visit* ***MelissaPortis.com*** *to request personalized support. Complete the short form under "Questions," and we'll reach out to help you get unstuck and get you back on track. Do that now and come right back to the book.*

THE REALM OF TRUTH

Welcome to chapter 7, where we're shaking things up with some real talk. We're all about creating spaces where authenticity reigns and vulnerability is celebrated. Ready to get into it? Let's go!

Create a Truth-Safe Zone: Foster Open Communication

Picture this: a space where you can say what's really on your mind without worrying about judgment. Sounds good, right? Creating a truth-safe zone is all about making that dream a reality. When you foster open communication, you not only invite honesty but also build trust that can handle anything. A partner who values transparency will be drawn to someone who's all about keeping it real and open.

Get the Real Talk Going: Be that friend who makes everyone feel comfortable to speak their truth.

Impact Moves

Be the emotional opener: Use warm vulnerability to invite truth. **Example:** "I love when people can just be real with me, it's refreshing."

- Ask evocative questions that open emotional doors, not just facts. "What's something that's been on your heart lately?"
- Set the tone with your presence, not just words. Calm energy invites truth.

Conversations that create "felt safety" in the brain where people feel seen, safe, and soothed stimulate integration in the nervous system. Meaning?

Emotionally safe dialogue promotes trust, connection, and intimacy.

Master This; The **"Truth Invite"** line:

"You don't have to filter with me. I like the unedited version." This helps him feel like he can drop the performance mask.

Listen Up: Show genuine interest in what others are saying, ditch the distractions.

Impact Moves

Use verbal mirroring: Repeat or rephrase something meaningful he says to show it landed. "So, it sounds like that was a huge shift for you…"

- Eliminate distractions during important convos, eye contact, and body language matter.
- Ask deepening questions, not topic changers.

Master This; The **"Echo + Expand"** listening technique:

- Echo back what he said
- Expand with a curious follow-up

Example: *"You said your dad taught you that, what was he like growing up?"*

Keep It Judgment Free: Make it a safe space where people can be honest without fear.

Impact Moves: Respond to vulnerability with validation, not fixing.

"I really respect you for sharing that."

- Watch for micro-expressions, raised eyebrows, or pursed lips can signal disapproval. Practice warmth and neutrality.
- **Normalize emotional expression:** "We all have layers, thank you for trusting me with that."

Master This; The **"No Fix, Just Feel"** rule:

When someone shares, resist the urge to solve. Just see and honor their experience.

That presence creates emotional depth and attraction.

Ditch the "Pretty Lies": Embrace Honesty

Let's be honest, those little "pretty lies" are like glitter. They might look cute at first, but they get everywhere and are impossible to clean up. Embracing honesty, even when it's awkward, is the way to go. It builds trust and keeps things real. Being truthful doesn't mean you have to be harsh; it's about having the courage to be upfront with a sprinkle of kindness. When you're all about honesty, you attract people who appreciate the real deal, not just the highlight reel.

Keep It Real: Speak your truth with kindness and maybe a dash of humor.

Impact Moves

Use clear statements with emotional intelligence: "Here's how I really feel, and I say this with all sincerity…"

- Include softening tones, warmth, playfulness, or humor so honesty feels safe, not sharp.
- **Validate first, then be honest:** "I see where you're coming from. And here's what's also true for me…"

Master This; The **"Love + Line" Model:**

Start with a sentiment of care or humor → then deliver the truth.

Example: "Okay, real talk. I like and respect you…but that didn't sit well with me." or being with you is like having my own superhero…. but rubbed me the wrong way.

Ditch the Sugar-Coating: Deliver your message straight up, no chaser.

Impact Moves

Match your tone with your truth: Say serious things seriously and light things lightly.

- **Replace passive language with direct phrases:** "I need..." instead of "I was just wondering…" "That doesn't work for me." instead of "I guess it's fine…"
- **Own your truth without apology:** "I want a deep connection, not surface stuff."

Master This; The **"Clarity Over Comfort"** rule**:**

If you're being unclear just to avoid discomfort, it's not communication, it's self-protection. Say what's real, respectfully.

Build That Trust: Honest vibes lead to solid, trusting relationships.

Impact Moves

Speak from grounded energy not reactivity. Before sharing truth, pause, breathe, and choose presence.

- **Show consistency between what you say and how you say it:** No mixed messages.
- **Follow honesty with curiosity:** "How does that land for you?"

Master This; The **“Say It, Then Soften It”** flow:

1. State the truth
2. Hold gentle eye contact
3. Open space for a response

This builds emotional safety and deepens connection, even when the conversation is real.

Studies show that the *tone of voice and facial expressions* during honest communication determines whether people feel safe or threatened. Trust is built when truth is delivered with calm and emotionally aligned energy.

Own Your Mess: Be Vulnerable and Courageous

Owning your mess is about saying, “This is me, take it or leave it.” It’s having the guts to be vulnerable and share your true self with the world. According to the self-disclosure theory, revealing idiosyncrasies (unique quirks or habits) and imperfections increases *perceived closeness and likability* in relationships. What you try to hide becomes the wall; what you reveal with confidence becomes the bridge. This level of authenticity is magnetic; it draws people in and encourages them to drop their masks too. By owning your mess, you're showing you're human, relatable, and so much more than perfect.

Embrace Your Quirks: Open up about your unique challenges and imperfections.

Impact Moves

Share quirky or awkward habits with playfulness: "I organize my spice rack by color, and smell, it's therapeutic for me!"

- **Normalize your insecurities by owning them confidently:** "I sweat so bad whenever I speak in front of a crowd; by the end of it, it looks like I went swimming!"
- **Lead with self-acceptance:** When she embraces it, others follow her cue.

Master This; Use the **"Quirk Drop"** technique early in conversations:

Sprinkle in a charming imperfection to break the perfection mask. This creates instant emotional permission for authenticity.

Share with Heart: Be bold in letting others see the real you, not just the highlight reel.

Impact Moves

Speak from "present truth," not rehearsed pain: "This is still something I'm learning to be okay with…"

- **Use emotional storytelling not trauma dumping:** Brief, honest stories with personal meaning are the sweet spot.
- **Pair honesty with self-trust:** "I'm proud of how I'm growing through this."

Master This; The **"60-Second Share"** method"

1. Name the challenge
2. Share one insight from it
3. End with where you are now emotionally

Short, heartfelt stories invite emotional intimacy without overwhelming the listener.

Deepen the Connection: Vulnerability invites authenticity and brings people closer.

Impact Moves

Let emotional tone match the moment: Be present and responsive, not overly polished.

- Make space for *his* emotional sharing after yours. This is key to reciprocity.
- **Reflect his shares back with warmth, not advice:** "Thank you for sharing that, it means a lot."

Master This; The **"Echo and Elevate"** practice in conversation:

Mirror what he shares and reflect something positive about his emotional truth.

"That's really grounded. I love how open you are about that."

🩶 Melissa's Personal Tip To Make Your King Melt 🩶

Say the hard thing with softness.

Use: "Hey babe, I want to open up about something important, and I feel we both can approach it with love and understanding".

CHAPTER
— *Eight* —

BUILDING YOUR KINGDOM

Welcome to Chapter 8, where we're all about building the life of your dreams and making it as fabulous as you are. This week, we're rewriting your story, kicking out those pesky doubts, and stepping into a future that's all yours. Ready to get started? Let's dive in!

Ghostwrite Your Future: Visualize Success

Alright, picture this: you're the writer of your own grand saga, and the ending is whatever you want it to be. Visualizing success isn't just about dreaming; it's about setting the scene for where you're headed. Think of it as your personal GPS when you know the destination, it's easier to figure out the route. Let me help you, there's a part of your brain, called the Reticular Activating System (RAS), basically it's a network of neurons located in the brain that locks onto what you feed it; so, if you're only looking at "bare minimum energy," guess what you'll find? Visual cues literally rewire your focus and magnetism. Spend a few minutes each day visualizing your goals in vivid detail to go beyond just the bare minimum. This isn't just daydreaming; it's setting the stage for your actions.

Trust me, when you see it clearly, the universe starts lining up the right opportunities.

A woman with a clear vision and purpose has it going on. Your confidence and direction will draw in a partner who respects and shares your dreams, creating a powerful dynamic duo.

Create Your Vision Board: Get creative with images and words that scream your goals.

Impact Moves

Put up images and words that scream *this is my energy*! Think about values, lifestyle, and how you want to feel.

- Add photos of you in your element, smiling like you own the room.
- Keep it somewhere you *can't* ignore, your brain eats what it sees.

Master This; The **"Image to Emotion"** link:

When you look at a vision board photo, *say out loud* the feeling it gives you. *"This is pure positive energy, I can see myself on this island already."*

Visualization fires up the same parts of your brain as real-life moments. That's why pro athletes use it because your brain can't tell if it's rehearsal or game day. When you rehearse confidence, you start living it.

Daily Visualization Time: Set aside a moment each day to picture your success story.

Impact Moves

Spend 3–5 minutes a day seeing yourself with your king. Not just what he looks like but how you *feel* around him.

- **Add sensory detail:** his voice, your laugh, where you're sitting, the way his eyes light up.
- Breathe deep while you do it, so it helps your nervous system associate attraction with a sense of calm.

Master This; The **"Echo Your Future Statement"**

Right after you visualize, drop a power line like it's already a fact. *"I'm magnetic around a man who truly values me."*

Map Out Your Goals: Break your vision into bite-sized, actionable steps.

Impact Moves

Break it down. **Weekly micro-goals:** talk to two new people, hit one social event, practice that subtle mirroring move once.

- Keep receipts, write it down so you can see your progress. Tiny wins pump dopamine through your system, which gives you a natural high that makes you want to keep pushing forward.
- If something's not working, tweak it. You're building data on what makes *your* chemistry click.

Master This; The **"Micro-Win Share"** habit:

Once a week, brag a little. Text a friend or someone you trust: *"Tried my playful lean-in move today, he was hooked."*

Edit Toxic Narratives: Reframe Limiting Beliefs

We all know that inner critic who loves to pop up saying "You can't do that." blah blah blah with all the negativity. Time to tell that voice to kick rocks.

Reframing limiting beliefs is about flipping the script and replacing those doubts with empowering truths.

When you catch yourself thinking negatively, counter it with a positive affirmation. This is about rewriting your mental playlist from "I can't" to "Watch me!"

Remember Philippians 4:13: "I can do all things through Christ who strengthens me." That's your new anthem!

When you've conquered your own doubts and stand firm in your beliefs you become irresistible. Your inner strength and self-assurance will draw in a partner of substance who values and admires your resilience.

Spot the Doubts: Jot down those pesky limiting beliefs.

Impact Moves

Keep a running list of every sneaky, negative thought about love, men, or yourself.

- Don't censor, write them exactly how they pop up.
- Recognize patterns (e.g., "Men always leave" or "I'm too much") this is so they stop running the show in the background.

Master This; The **"Truth Bomb Test"**

When a doubt shows up, ask: *"Would I teach this belief to a friend or child?"* If not, get rid of it immediately and replace it with a positive thought.

Flip the Script: Turn them into positive affirmations.

Impact Moves

Rewrite each limiting belief into a bold, loving, present-tense statement.

- Keep the wording short and powerful so your brain can latch onto it.
- **Make it about identity, not just action:** *"I am a confident, loving, and caring woman"* not *"I will try to be confident." Get rid of the word "TRY".*

Master This; The **"Mirror Mic Drop"**

Say the affirmation in the mirror with the exact tone you'd use if you were hyping up your best friend.

Empower Your Mindset: Keep those affirmations on repeat to reinforce new beliefs.

Impact Moves

Repeat affirmations out loud 2–3 times a day, ideally in moments when you feel good.

- Pair affirmations with music, movement, or scent so your brain anchors them to pleasure.
- Use them *before* dates or social events to heightened confidence.

Master This; The **"Loop It Like a Hook"** technique:

Record yourself saying the affirmations over a beat you love and play it like a playlist while getting ready or in the car on your way to work.

Cast Yourself as the Lead: Reclaim Power from Past Pain

Every action movie needs a hero, and guess what? You're the star of this show! Casting yourself as the lead means taking back your power from past pain and strutting confidently into your role as the main character. This is about owning your journey, embracing your resilience, and letting past experiences fuel you to want better for yourself. By choosing to be the lead in your story, you're setting the stage for decisions that align with your dreams and values.

A woman who owns her story and walks with purpose is captivating. Your journey of overcoming challenges makes you relatable and inspiring, attracting a partner who appreciates your depth and strength.

Reflect on Past Pain: Acknowledge what you've been through and the strength it's given you.

Impact Moves

Write down the key moments that shaped "love" for you, both the heartbreaks and the breakthroughs.

- Note the strengths each challenge built in your (patience, boundaries, and emotional depth).
- **Say it out loud:** *"I survived that, and I'm stronger because of it."*

When you name your experiences and the emotions tied to them, you activate the hippocampus (memory processing) and the prefrontal cortex (decision making), which helps your brain file it as "resolved" instead of "unresolved"

Master This: "Journal Mapping" technique:

1. Journal 5 minutes focusing on growth, not pain.
2. Map your love timeline with lessons learned.
3. Say: *"My past pain shows my strength."*

Embrace Your Resilience: Let your past be a steppingstone, not a stumbling block.

Impact Moves

Transform setbacks into stories of growth by sharing lessons learned with authenticity.

- *Respond to challenges with calm confidence, not reactive defensiveness.*
- *Hold space for vulnerability and strength simultaneously, own your emotions without letting them control you.*

Master This: "Rewrite to Rise" technique:

- Add a positive phrase of you overcoming tough memories.

- Keep your wins in a journal near you to boost confidence.
- Thank yourself silently for resilience.

Lead Your Story: Make choices that reflect your values and aspirations.

Impact Moves

Identify and clearly articulate your top 3 relationship values (e.g., honesty, growth, kindness).

- Filter your decisions and conversations through these values, ensuring consistency and authenticity.
- Use firm but graceful boundary setting language to protect your values and priorities.

Stand On This Standard:

1. Value shapes behavior.
2. Behavior shapes trust.
3. Trust shapes love.

Master This; Frame conversations with a 3-part values rhythm:

1. **Value Statement** – "I really value honesty in my relationships…" (sets clear expectations)
2. **Personal Reflection** – "That's why I've learned to trust actions over words…" (builds credibility)
3. **Engaging Boundary/Question** – "How do you show honesty in your relationships?" (invites meaningful dialogue)

🩶 Melissa's Personal Tip To Make Your King Melt 🩶

Show him how you've grown.

Reveal something like,

"There was a time where I would have flown off the handle in this situation. You don't have to worry; I'll never go back to that place in my life ever again because our relationship means more than anything to me".

That evolution is magnetic. It tells him you're not repeating old cycles.

Feeling stuck? *If you're reading this and thinking, "I have no idea how to move forward," don't worry! We've got your back. Visit* ***MelissaPortis.com*** *to request personalized support. Complete the short form under "Questions," and we'll reach out to help you get unstuck and get you back on track. Do that now and come right back to the book.*

THE ART OF INTIMACY

Welcome to Chapter 9, where we're diving into the juicy art of intimacy. We're talking about baring your soul, getting cozy, and vibing on a spiritual wavelength with your partner. Ready to level up in love? Let's dive in!

Bare Your Soul: Cultivate Emotional Intimacy

Alright, emotional intimacy is all about peeling back those layers and letting someone in. It's sharing your dreams, your fears, and all the bits that make you, well, you. When you bare your soul, you're creating a vibe that's all about trust and connection. Proverbs 27:19 hits home with this: "As water reflects the face, so one's life reflects the heart." Your openness is like a magnet, pulling your partner in and building a bond that's rock solid. When we open up and share our feelings with others, something fascinating happens in our brains, we release oxytocin, often called the "bonding hormone."

It's like our brains are wired to connect when we're vulnerable with each other. And the best part is, this isn't just a one-time thing! Relationship experts have found that being consistently open with the people we care about helps create deeper and more secure bonds over time.

Share Your Heart: Be that open book about your feelings and dreams.

Impact Moves

Share your feelings and dreams in ways that are heartfelt but concise (avoid overwhelming detail, think depth over length).

- **Use language that blends emotion with vision:** "I've always dreamed of…" or "What matters most to me is…"
- Encourage a space where he feels safe to open up to respond to his vulnerability with curiosity, not critique.

Invite Vulnerability: Encourage your partner to share their inner world, too.

Impact Moves

Lead with warmth and non-judgment: frame your curiosity as admiration ("I love hearing what shaped you").

- Ask open-ended, emotionally safe questions: "What's something you've learned the hard way, but wouldn't trade?"
- Reward his openness; respond with validation, not advice ("That makes sense… I appreciate you sharing that with me.").

Master This; The **"Step-Down Approach"**

Share a small personal truth, pause then ask his perspective. It's a gentle way to invite him in without pressure.

Build Trust: Keep that emotional sharing going to strengthen trust.

A king loves a partner who's emotionally available and ready to share their world. Your vulnerability is a superpower that draws him in and deepens your connection. Behavioral psychology and attachment theory show that consistent emotional responsiveness strengthens secure bonding; a pattern of it showing up in small, meaningful ways

Impact Moves

Treat every moment you share as an open door: Follow up later ("That trip you mentioned, how's the planning going?").

- **Match his level of disclosure:** balance openness without oversharing too soon.
- **Affirm reliability:** small, consistent actions build credibility faster than big gestures.

Master This; The **"Echo Statements"**

Reflect back key phrases he shares ("Sounds like family means a lot to you"), to make him feel truly heard and deepen trust.

Skin Deep: Foster Physical Intimacy

Physical intimacy isn't just about the sex, it's about creating a safe, loving space. It's the soft touch, the warm hugs, and the feeling of being connected. This kind of intimacy says, "I'm here, I care," and it's a beautiful way to show love. It's not just about the attraction; it's about feeling united and cherished.

Create Comfort: Make sure that physical touch is all about comfort and care.

Impact Moves

Use touch as a grounding tool, think slow and steady rather than quick or intense.

- Focus on shared moments of laughter or calm; these amplify the soothing effect.
- Let touch be an invitation, not an expectation signal, "I enjoy being near you," rather than "I need something from you."

Master This; The **"Shoulder Rule":** a brief touch on the shoulder or upper back is universally read as warm and reassuring, perfect for building safety without going overboard.

Explore Together: Find out what feels good and comforting for both of you.

Impact Moves

Use curious language: "I love how we figure out what feels natural for us."

- Experiment slowly; change pace, pressure, or context and notice what brings mutual ease.
- Frame physical closeness as collaboration, not performance: celebrate what works instead of overanalyzing what doesn't.

A king appreciates a partner who brings warmth to their shared moments, enhancing the bond with authenticity.

Master This; The **"Notice Name Nurture"** sequence:

- **Notice:** Tune into your own body and emotions first.
- **Name:** Put clear, simple words to what you're feeling.
- **Nurture:** Invite him into the process with a caring suggestion such as "*Hey, how about we cook dinner together sometime? I'd love to see what we could whip up in the kitchen!"*

Express Affection: Use those little touches to show love and appreciation.

Impact Moves

Give your partner a warm hug during everyday moments like when one of you is heading out the door or switching rooms in the house.

- Use a mix of verbal and nonverbal cues ("I love this about you" paired with a playful touch).
- Treat affection as ongoing dialogue, not an isolated event.

This approach keeps affection dynamic rather than routine. Behavioral science shows that *variable reinforcement* (small, delightful surprises) keeps emotional connection exciting and keeps your partner wanting more.

Master This; The **"Touch Tag Tune"** exercise**:**

- **Touch:** Initiate a brief, loving gesture (hand squeeze).
- **Tag:** Pair it with a one-line affirmation ("Being with you is like an adventure," "I love seeing you happy").
- **Tune:** Watch how he responds, lean in more if he lights up, keep it simple if he's distracted.

A king is drawn to a queen who embraces both physical and mental closeness, expressing love in diverse and meaningful ways. Your openness to connect respectfully keeps the relationship vibrant and full of love. Research shows that even just a few seconds of affectionate gestures such as eye contact with a smile and a quick brush of the hand creates measurable physiological synchrony between partners' heart rates and breathing. This rhythm literally makes two people feel more "in tune."

Spiritual Intimacy & Shared Values: Align on a Soul Level

Spiritual intimacy is where the magic happens. It's about connecting on a deeper level, aligning your values, beliefs, and dreams for the future. When you share spiritual intimacy, you're building a relationship of respect and understanding. It's that unshakeable foundation that sees you through life's ups and downs.

Share Beliefs: Get into what you both believe and how it guides your lives.

Impact Moves

Talk about beliefs as guiding lights, not dividing lines: Instead of "I only date men who believe what I believe," try "Faith is what helps me stay grounded and joyful. What keeps you balanced and aligned?"

- **Use stories, not lectures:** Share a moment when your belief shaped your choice, rather than just stating the belief itself.

- **Lead with curiosity:** “What experiences shaped what you believe?” creates dialogue instead of debate.

Master This; The **“Story Spark”** technique:

Share a short (60–90 second) story about a belief that matters to you.

End with a question: “"Tell me, has there been a moment in your life that has impacted you?" This invites a deeper connection and encourages understanding and it creates connection instead of confrontation.

A king is looking for a partner who can vibe with him on many levels. Your shared values and spiritual connection are the bedrock of a love that lasts.

Align Values: Make sure your core values are in sync.

Impact Moves

Pay attention to his actions, not just what he says.

- **Use empowering language:** “I’m drawn to people who value loyalty and kindness,” instead of saying “I won’t date liars.”

- **Ask value-based questions early:** "What matters most to you?"

Master This; The **"Value Map"** exercise**:**

- Name your top three core values (e.g., growth, faith, adventure).
- Ask him and see where they overlap or complement.
- Focus on alignment as synergy (togetherness), not sameness.

Vision Together: Dream up a shared future that reflects your spiritual bond.

Impact Moves

Paint a picture of where you want to be in life, as fun and inspiring, not a pressure.

- **Use future focused questions:** "If you could design your perfect day, what would it look like?"
- **Share dreams in a way that invites partnership:** "I've always imagined…." what's your dream?"

Master This; "Paint the Picture" method**:**

Share one vivid detail about your ideal future.

- **Ask him to add a brushstroke:** "What would you add to make it perfect?"
- Keep it playful and creative, vision bonding should feel exciting, not heavy.

 Melissa's Personal Tip To Make Your King Melt 🩶

Be gentle and mysterious.

"Imagine you're in a really engaging conversation, and the vibe is just right. Sit close to him, place your hand behind his neck, smile and give a gentle rub before slowly moving your hand away. Maintain eye contact throughout to deepen the connection".

UNVEILING YOUR DESTINY

Welcome to Chapter 10, where we're all about aligning with your true path and embracing the journey ahead.

This chapter is your guide to becoming irresistibly aligned with your destiny, setting unapologetic boundaries, and realizing that growth is the ultimate gamechanger. Ready to step into your future with confidence? Let's dive in!

Elevate Your Appeal: Align with Your Destiny

When you align with your destiny, you naturally elevate your appeal. It's like stepping into your power and letting your true self shine through. When you're on the right path, everything starts to click into place, and that confidence is magnetic. Knowing who you are and where you're going not only attracts the right people into your life but also enhances every aspect of your being. And here's the kicker: a king is drawn to a queen who is confident and knows her path. Your alignment with your destiny makes you irresistible to a partner who values authenticity and purpose.

Identify Your Path: Reflect on what truly excites and motivates you.

Impact Moves

Speak about your desires as values, not demands: "I love meaningful conversation" instead of "I hate small talk."

- Catch yourself if you feel you're performing for approval, pause and ask, "Is this really me?"
- **Frame your story as a journey, not a sales pitch:** share where you're growing, not just where you shine.

Master This; The **"Truth Test"**

- **Before saying yes, posting, or committing, ask:** *Would I still choose this if nobody celebrated me for it?*
- If yes, it's authentic. If no, it's performance.

Set Intentions: Align your daily actions with your long-term goals.

Impact Moves

Start your day with a grounding ritual (meditation, journaling) to activate intention and serotonin.

- **Visualize your future self and ask:** *"What would I do today?"* This stimulates dopamine and focus.
- Track small wins to reinforce progress (reward centers in the brain respond to mini accomplishments).
- Celebrate follow-through (even imperfect) to build inner trust and oxytocin.

Master This; The **3-Part Daily Intention:**

1. **Warm intention:** "Today I choose to…" (directs attention + behavior)
2. **Personal meaning:** "Because this brings me closer to…" (links action to purpose)
3. **Check-in:** "How will I feel after doing this?" (engages emotional alignment)

Embrace Authenticity: Let your true self guide your journey.

Impact Moves

Speak from inner truth: *"What matters to me is..." or "Something I value in connection is..."*

- **Replace self-editing with self-honoring:** *"Here's how I really feel about that."*
- **Use "graceful truth" phrases:** *"That's not quite what I'm into, but I appreciate the offer."*

Master This; The "**Real Over Polished**" rule:

When in doubt, share something real rather than trying to say it perfectly. Say "This might sound random, but..." "To keep it real with you, this is what it is right now..." "I don't have an answer, but here's where I'm at..."

Unapologetic Boundaries: Establish Firm Boundaries

Setting boundaries is all about respecting yourself and your needs. Unapologetic boundaries mean you're clear about what you will and won't accept. This clarity is attractive because it shows confidence and self-respect.

A partner who values and respects you will be drawn to someone who knows her worth and isn't afraid to stand by it. Establishing firm boundaries tells the world that you're not settling for anything less than you deserve.

Know Your Limits: Identify what's non-negotiable for you.

Impact Moves

Stick to your guns without wavering, even when challenged.

- Expect discomfort at first, it's a sign of growth, not guilt.
- Use calm repetition and disengagement if needed.

Master this; The "**Boundary Reset"** method:

Repeat your boundary calmly, don't debate it. Say, "I've already shared where I stand." *(Then pause and stay silent.)*

Communicate Clearly: Express your boundaries with confidence and respect.

Impact Moves

Use calm, direct language, skip over explaining.

- Replace "I'm sorry" with "Thank you for understanding."
- Express limits in a way that honors both yourself and his.

Master This; The **"Bold N Sweet"** technique:

Use short, warm statements to express your needs, no apologies, no over explaining.

Say, "That doesn't work for me, but I appreciate the ask."

This keeps boundaries clear while staying kind and composed.

Stand Firm: Enforce your boundaries consistently.

Master This; The **"10 Toes Down Method"**

You meant what you said!

Growth Is Sexy: Embrace Growth for Long-Term Success

Let's be real, growth is sexy. Embracing personal development and being open to change keeps you moving forward. Behavioral psychology research reveals that when we develop a growth mindset;

believing in our abilities, relationships can develop. It activates the brain's anterior cingulate cortex (helps sort through details) and prefrontal cortex (helps you focus on what really matters), improving emotional regulation, and resilience. Viewing challenges as growth opportunities reduces threat responses in the brain and boosts learning from setbacks. Growth isn't just about achieving goals; it's about evolving and becoming the best version of yourself. This journey is incredibly attractive because it shows resilience and adaptability. A king who values growth will be drawn to a partner who is constantly striving to better herself.

Your commitment to growth tells him that you're in it for the long haul and ready to build a successful future together.

Commit to Learning: Always be open to new experiences and knowledge.

Impact Moves

Approach finding your king, your destiny partner as a journey, not a test.

- Ask open-ended questions that invite new perspectives.

- **Reflect after each interaction:** "What did I learn about myself or him today?"

Master This; Stay curious by trying phrases like:

- "I'm curious about…"
- "Help me understand…"
- "What's something new you've discovered lately?"

Embrace Change: See challenges as opportunities for growth.

Impact Moves

- **Reframe difficulties as valuable feedback, not failure.**

Example to practice: **After a bad date, say** "That showed me what I *don't* want; and that's just as important."

Celebrate Progress: Acknowledge and celebrate your achievements.

✨🩶✨ Melissa's Personal Tip To Make Your King Melt ✨🩶✨

Genuine compliment with a playful hint.

Say,

"I love your fit, you look so handsome (smile).

You must have known purple is my favorite color".

Feeling stuck? *If you're reading this and thinking, "I have no idea how to move forward," don't worry! We've got your back. Visit* ***MelissaPortis.com*** *to request personalized support. Complete the short form under "Questions," and we'll reach out to help you get unstuck and get you back on track. Do that now and come right back to the book.*

OWN IT! YOU ARE GODS

Welcome to Chapter 11, where we're tapping into that divine energy and owning our worth like the gods and goddesses we are. Irresistible isn't a look, it's a vibe.

It's that quiet confidence that radiates from within. No pretending, no begging for approval, and definitely no settling for less. When you own your worth, you stop convincing people to choose you, you let them earn a spot in your story. Trust me, the right ones will sprint through fire just to meet you there.

Clarity as Your Crown

Wearing clarity as your crown means you're deciding the fate of your relationship by defining exactly what you will and won't tolerate. This clarity acts like a spiritual sieve, weeding out distractions and aligning you with partnerships that mirror your purpose. The result? A regal energy! You stop justifying, overexplaining, or shrinking. Instead, you step into spaces like you've unlocked life's cheat code, radiating a quiet certainty that says, "I'm not chasing love, I'm the catch."

Define Your Standards: Clearly outline what you expect and need in a relationship.

Impact Moves

Attraction Audit: Compare relationship traits of "hot-but-harmful" versus "calm-and-connected" relationships to identify security promoting qualities.

- **Highlight Security Traits:** Focus on traits like consistency and accountability that align with emotional safety.
- **Behavioral Indicators:** Convert needs into observable behaviors, such as "respect" being demonstrated by keeping plans and clarifying intentions within 48 hours.
- **Visualize Secure Dating:** Think of being with a king that's secure mentally, financially, and that's fun loving. Visualize new experiences like something as simple as laughter, to recondition excitement toward safety.

When doing these impact moves, be real with yourself about what you truly want and need in a man. Here's the thing, our attachment history and that pesky dopamine salience bias that can trick us into mistaking drama for chemistry. When we're clear on our standards upfront, we save ourselves from those mental gymnastics of justifying red flags.

Master This; Use the **"Value-Reveal Story Structure"**

Share something significant with him.

- Highlight how it shaped you.
- Tie it to a core value.

A purposeful partner resonates with you, while a misaligned partner never goes deeper than surface level.

Align with Purpose: Seek partnerships that reflect your interests, not just his.

Impact Moves

- **Ping-pong prompts:** "If we had the entire weekend free, what would we plan?"

- **Callback to earlier aims:** “You mentioned fitness, want to try going to the track next week for a run?”
- **Target:** One small **co-plan** within 2–3 dates.

Master This:

1. When he offers plans: pause, smile, receive, then refine “Love that, Tuesday works better.”
2. Use silence strategically; let him take initiative, then reward with warmth.

Micro-cue: Head tilt + “Mmm, I like that idea.”

Radiate Confidence: Walk with the assurance that you are the prize.

Impact Moves

Hold steady eye contact and relaxed shoulders when entering a room your presence arrives before your words.

- Speak decisively using upward energy at the start of sentences and a grounded tone at the close (shows both warmth and authority).
- Acknowledge your own wins out loud without deflecting or minimizing them.

Master This; The **"Magnetic Posture"** formula:

Aligned spine + deliberate pauses before responding + slow smile = effortless high-value energy.

1. **Practice a power walk drill:** At home, walk toward a mirror holding eye contact with yourself, no fidgeting, no downward glance.
2. **Compliment acceptance practice:** When someone praises her, respond with "Thank you, I receive that".
3. **Pause mastery:** In conversation, count "one-two" silently before answering a question to train unhurried presence.

Being confident (not cocky) sends a powerful message to high value men. Research shows we're naturally drawn to people who believe in themselves, since it suggests they have their act together. When you carry yourself with quiet self-assurance, it tells your partner "I know my worth" and that makes them value you more too.

Growth as an Aphrodisiac

Stagnant relationships dull your shine, while destiny-aligned choices polish it. When you prioritize growth over comfort, you become a walking testament to transformation. Your conversations shift from gossip to goals, and your habits from escapism to expansion.

People are hardwired to crave drive and determination; the pursuit of better makes you irresistible to those hungry to level up in their own lives.

Embrace Change: Welcome challenges as opportunities for growth.

Impact Moves

Share stories about obstacles reframed as *launchpads*, not losses.

- Demonstrate curiosity rather than fear when something unexpected happens.
- **Use forward-looking language:** "This is teaching me…" instead of "This is ruining me."

Master This; The "Adaptive Aura"

Calm breath + open chest posture + optimistic reframing = effortless magnetism under pressure.

Unexpected switch drill: Change something small (route to work, coffee order)

- **Journal:** Write a one-sentence about your gains from any setback within 24 hours.
- **Social cue test:** In conversation, share a recent challenge; something small. Pay attention to his demeanor and to see if he leans in, if so, he has a (growth mindset) or if he pulls away (fixed mindset).

Focus on Goals: Let your conversations and actions reflect your ambitions.

Impact Moves

Mention your pursuits naturally, without overexplaining, confidence makes goals self-evident.

- Align daily (calendar, routine) with big-picture vision.
- Surround yourself with people who normalize excellence, not excuses.

Master This; The "Subtle Signal" method:

Clear priorities + small evidence of progress + zero over-apology = goals that magnetize respect.

1. **"One-line vision" drill:** Practice summarizing your main goal in one powerful sentence.

2. **Filter check:** After a date, ask "Does this move me closer or farther from my goal?"
3. **Value anchor:** When someone asks about free time, mention an ambition-linked habit (e.g., "I feel most energized when I'm making progress on something meaningful.)

Research shows that when you speak about your aspirations with clarity, those around you who are actively listening, subconsciously align with your drive.

High value men naturally mirror ambition they find inspiring.

Inspire Others: Your drive attracts those who seek to grow alongside you.

Impact Moves

Speak about what excites you, not just about your dislikes, doing so can give off an impression that you're negative or critical; it's all about balance.

- Let people see small steps toward her goals, it signals consistency and self-respect.
- Don't be a hater; celebrate other people's wins, high value energy attracts high value men.

Master This; The **"Spark Effect"** formula:

Upward vocal inflection + animated facial expression + specific language about *why* you care = presence that naturally inspires.

- **Passion rep:** Record yourself talking about a project for 30 seconds. Add 10% more energy than feels normal, listen back and note how magnetic it sounds.
- **Momentum mention:** In conversations, drop one current thing you're working on in a way that feels casual, not forced.
- **Shared spotlight:** Call out someone else's growth publicly, this shows that you're confident in your own worth and supportive of others' successes, demonstrating leadership and grace.

Purpose as the Ultimate Attraction

Destiny-focused relationships transcend fleeting chemistry. You king will seek you out and amplify your purpose and not just your ego. This shift turns romance into a collaboration. You'll start building a legacy together! In a world obsessed with instant gratification, your commitment to a meaningful purpose becomes a beautiful song to those ready to trade drama for destiny.

Seek Alignment: Find partners who share or support your vision.

Impact Moves

Seek partners who naturally support your ambitions instead of tolerating them.

- Frame early conversations around vision, not just chemistry.
- Evaluate not just how he treats you now, but how he talks about the future.

Master This; The **"Future Him Test"**

1. Share a goal or dream out loud.
2. Watch how he responds, does he get curious, excited, or dismissive?
3. If he leans in, go deeper. If he deflects, take note, alignment starts here.

Build Together: Collaborate on creating a shared legacy.

Impact Moves

Choose shared projects or a business that reflect both your values.

- Celebrate small wins together to reinforce your partnership.
- Focus on "we" language: *"What are we building?"* instead of using "I" language.

Master This; The **"Mini Mission"** method:

1. Pick a small, shared goal (plan a trip, co-host a dinner) together.
2. Divide roles clearly but with flexibility (household chores, planning dates, financial management).
3. Celebrate completion even if it's a small task or getting the fridge cleaned or getting the laundry washed, folded, and put away.

Say: "I love when we work on__ together, it feels like we're building something bigger than just us."

Keep your tone playful and warm to avoid it sounding like pressure.

Lean in physically when sharing ideas your body language signals "I'm with you."

Studies in social psychology show that couples who pursue joint projects, whether financial, creative, or community-focused experience deeper intimacy and long-term satisfaction. Building something meaningful together triggers the brain's reward circuitry, bonding you like partners in adventure.

Commit to Purpose: Let your relationship be a testament to shared goals and dreams.

Impact Moves

Check whether his long-term direction complements yours.

- Make purposeful conversations a regular thing, not just a "big talk."
- Align decisions (career moves, location, lifestyle) with a shared "core value."

Master This; The **"Dream Alignment Check-in"**

1. **Once a month, ask:** *"What's exciting you right now about your future?"*
2. Share your own evolving vision honestly.
3. Identify common interests and discuss ways to cultivate them together.

Couples who articulate and revisit shared dreams consistently report stronger emotional intimacy and resilience. A relationship anchored to purpose becomes a partnership rather than just a romance.

Reflection and Action

As you embrace this chapter, take a moment to reflect on Psalm 82:6: "I said, 'You are gods; you are all sons of the Most High.'" What does this mean to you? What is God, the universe, or your inner being saying to you?

Create a Timeline: Outline achievable steps you plan to take within your current or future relationships.

Impact Moves

Define what you want in 6 months, 1 year, 3 years then communicate it to him clearly.

- Avoid rigid deadlines (they create pressure) and focus on direction instead.
- Treat milestones (anniversary of your first date by revisiting the same restaurant where it all began, reflecting on your journey). Use this as a checkpoint to confirm mutual alignment, not ultimatums.

Master This; The **"Relationship Roadmap"**

1. List three relationship goals (e.g., deeper trust, shared experiences, long-term commitment).
2. Assign a realistic timeframe to each without overloading the process.
3. **Check in with your partner:** *"Does this feel natural to you too?"*

Practice saying calmly*:* *"I like knowing where we're headed. What does that look like for you?"*

- Keep shoulders back, chin relaxed, your body says, *"I'm confident, not clingy."*
- **Use light humor to diffuse tension if the topic feels heavy**: *"No pressure, just mapping things out so we don't drive in circles."*

Listen to Your Inner Voice: What is it guiding you to do next?

Impact Moves

Notice how your body reacts in conversations, tightness often signals misalignment.

- **Ask yourself regularly:** *"Does this relationship allow me to grow or shrink me?"*

- Use journaling or voice notes to capture gut impressions in real time.

Master This; The **"Intuition Check"** formula:

1. Before making a big decision, sit quietly and name what you're feeling but don't analyze yet.
2. Write down three possible next steps and rate which feels most peaceful, not just most exciting.
3. Revisit later to see if your gut still says the same thing, consistency signals clarity.

✨🩶✨ Melissa's Personal Tip To Make Your King Melt ✨🩶✨

Embody the Essence of Commitment.

Say it like you mean it!

"Loving you feels so right. Babe, this isn't just a relationship God put us together for a purpose bigger than us."

A man melts when he feels your love as sacred.

CONCLUSION

YOUR JOURNEY TO ATTRACTING YOUR KING

We've journeyed through quite the adventure together, from unmasking those inner devils to building an irresistible kingdom where you reign supreme. Let's tie it all together with a beautiful bow and see how each step has paved the way to attracting your king. Ready to wrap it up with a dash of fun, a sprinkle of spiritual wisdom, and a whole lot of truth? Let's go!

The Royal Roadmap

Throughout this journey, you've been peeling back layers and unearthing the queen within. From owning your ugly truth (because, let's face it, we all have that baggage) to setting unapologetic boundaries that scream self-respect, you've been crafting a life and mindset that naturally draws in a high-value partner. Your ability to bare your soul cultivates emotional intimacy that's a magnet for genuine connection.

The Power of Connection

Emotional, physical, and spiritual intimacy each plays a role in creating a bond that's not just skin deep, but soul-deep. You've learned to communicate openly, ditch those "pretty lies," and embrace vulnerability.

This authenticity is like a beacon, attracting a partner who values honesty and depth. And let's not forget about the spiritual alignment, where shared values create a rock-solid foundation for a love that lasts.

Your Personal Come Up

Your commitment to personal growth and aligning with your destiny makes you shine brighter than ever.

Growth isn't just sexy; it's essential for long-term success. By continuously evolving, you become the kind of person who not only attracts the right partner but also builds a future filled with potential and purpose. Your story of resilience and empowerment invites a king who's ready to build a kingdom with you. \

Faith and Favor

Let's not forget the divine touch guiding this journey.

Your path is beautifully unique, and as you align with your purpose, you invite blessings and opportunities that resonate with your spirit. Proverbs 3:5-6 reminds us to "Trust in the Lord with all your heart and lean not on your own understanding; in all your ways submit to him, and he will make your paths straight." Remember, your journey is divinely guided, be in alignment and your king will be drawn to the light and love you exude.

Get ready to step boldly into your destiny and attract the love you deserve!

Feeling stuck? *If you're reading this and thinking, "I have no idea how to move forward," don't worry! We've got your back. Visit* ***MelissaPortis.com*** *to request personalized support. Complete the short form under "Questions," and we'll reach out to help you get unstuck and get you back on track. Do that now and come right back to the book.*

💔 The C.H.A.R.M. Method™ for Communication Based Attraction

Here's the bonus you've been waiting for! "The C.H.A.R.M. Method™ for Communication Based Attraction" is the cherry on top of everything you've soaked up in this book. It's like the ultimate roadmap that ties together all the juicy insights and wisdom you've encountered, helping you attract and be drawn to the right man through emotionally intelligent communication. Think of it as a God given nudge toward building connections that truly matter, all while keeping it fun, real, and spiritually grounded. With this framework, you'll learn to spark chemistry, embrace vulnerability, align values, create a reciprocity loop, and radiate a magnetic feminine presence. Ready to make those connections sizzle?

C – Chemistry (Neuro-Based Communication)

Science Insight: Chemistry isn't just "spark" it's the neurochemical cocktail of oxytocin (bonding), dopamine (desire), and serotonin (safety).

✅ **Coaching Focus:** Use warm eye contact, vocal tone, and presence to activate oxytocin.

- **Ask dopamine-triggering questions:** "What lights you up lately?"
- Mirror gestures or posture subtly to create familiarity and resonance (chameleon effect).

🧠 **Tool**: The **3-Part Spark Sentence**

1. "I noticed…" (engages attention)
2. "That reminds me of…" (personal connection)
3. "What's your take on…?" (emotional reciprocity)

H – Heart-Centered Vulnerability

Science Insight: Vulnerability, when shared skillfully, releases oxytocin and creates emotional safety and intimacy (based on Dr. Brene Brown's research).

✅ **Coaching Focus:** Share short emotional truths not to overshare, but to open doors.

- Use "vulnerability probes" to gauge connection: "I really value depth, how does that land for you?"
- Speak in "I" statements that show ownership without blame.

🧠 **Tool**: The **Heartbeat Model**

1. Open – Share a real moment
2. Invite – "Has that ever happened to you?"
3. Reflect – "That makes sense. I love how you think about that."

A – Alignment of Values & Styles

Science Insight: Lasting attraction depends on compatibility in **core values**, communication style, and lifestyle rhythm not just chemistry.

✅ **Coaching Focus: Ask layered questions:** "How do you like to resolve conflict?" or "What's your ideal day off?"

- Watch how he processes emotions (external vs. internal processors).

- **Share her own values early:** “I care deeply about honesty and play what about you?”

Tool: The **Values Ladder**

Start light → Explore lifestyle → Go deep into beliefs (e.g., family, growth, partnership dynamics)

R – Reciprocity Loop

Science Insight: Reciprocity builds trust and engagement, emotional giving and receiving wires the brain for closeness.

Coaching Focus: Balance emotional shares with curiosity. “That changed how I see love. What about you?”

- Practice call-backs: refer to something he said earlier to show attunement.
- Match emotional depth not just words.

Tool: The **Ping-Pong Principle**

Create flow through equal parts sharing, listening, and reflecting. No monologues build emotional rhythm.

M – Magnetic Feminine Presence

Science Insight: Nonverbal signals (body language, tone, and presence) account for up to 93% of emotional communication. The feminine energy of openness, softness, and emotional grounding is deeply attractive.

✅ **Coaching Focus:** Breathe into her body, slow her speech, and smile with intention.

- Use "open signals" relaxed arms, curved posture, face turned toward him.
- Communicate warmth + boundaries simultaneously ("I'd love that / That doesn't feel aligned").

🧠 **Tool**: The **Feminine Frequency Checklist**

- Eye contact
- Slow gestures
- Grounded tone
- Expressive face
- Presence over performance

The ALIGN Method ⚖️

Core Premise: People pleasing isn't kindness, its self-abandonment rooted in fear of rejection.

When you learn to ALIGN (Awareness, Love, Inner security, Genuine boundaries, high standards), then you stop over giving and start receiving which attracts men who value and respect you.

A — Awareness of Your Pattern

Science Insight: Neuroscience research shows chronic people-pleasing is tied to an overactive *anterior cingulate cortex* (the brain's "social pain center"), which creates anxiety at the slightest hint of conflict.

✅ **Coaching Focus:** Identify when you say "yes" to avoid discomfort rather than from genuine desire.

- Use attachment theory tools to spot whether you lean anxious, avoidant, or secure.
- Track moments when you shrink, apologize excessively, or downplay your needs.

Micro-Rehearsal: Practice a soft smile + steady eye contact when saying *"Let me think about that"* instead of an automatic *"Sure!"*.

L — Love Your Authentic Self

Science Insight: Self-acceptance boosts oxytocin and serotonin chemicals linked to emotional stability and secure bonding.

✅ **Coaching Focus:** Shift from external validation to internal self-regard.

- Use daily affirmations that reinforce *"I'm worthy even when I'm not accommodating everyone."*
- Rewrite your self-story: from "I'm liked because I'm easy" → "I'm loved because I'm real."

Micro-Rehearsal: Mirror exercise: Look at yourself and say, *"My desires matter."*

This rewires the brain's reward pathways around self-recognition.

I — Inner Security First

Science Insight: Strong vagal tone (part of your parasympathetic nervous system) is linked to emotional resilience and the ability to stay calm in conflict.

✅ **Coaching Focus:** Learn grounding techniques (breathwork, body language resets) to stay centered even when others disapprove.

- Build emotional regulation practices that replace the need to control others' reactions.

Micro-Rehearsal: Before dates or tough conversations, do a 4-7-8 breathing cycle to calm your nervous system.

G — Genuine Boundaries

Science Insight: Healthy boundaries signal high value men, behavioral psychology research shows people subconsciously respect those who calmly enforce limits.

✅ **Coaching Focus:** Replace fear-based "walls" with love-based standards.

- **Use communication scripts that are warm yet firm:** *"I care about you, but this doesn't work for me."*

- Role play scenarios where you say no without guilt.

Micro-Rehearsal: Practice an open posture while declining something shoulders relaxed, hands visible to communicate calm power.

N — Noble Standards in Love

Science Insight: Biology shows high value partners instinctively gravitate toward those who signal self-respect and discernment not compliance.

✅ **Coaching Focus:** Define what kind of treatment you will and will not accept.

- Use relationship vision mapping to ensure alignment before investing emotionally.
- Choose partners who meet you at your level rather than rescuing or proving yourself.

Micro-Rehearsal: Script out your *"I'm looking for a relationship where..."* statement and say it out loud until it feels natural.

Practice

1. **Diagnostic phase:** Identify your people-pleasing triggers using real-life examples.
2. **Step-by-step rewiring:** Take one letter of ALIGN per week (or per session) and practice micro-rehearsals.
3. **Integration phase:** Test these tools in low stakes situations (friends, coworkers) before dating scenarios.
4. **Attraction phase:** Learn to respect your strengths and observe which men lean in (healthy ones) vs. pull away (users) a great filter method.

ACKNOWLEDGMENTS

To my partner, my king, my blessing, Kevin.

This book would not exist without you. You are not only the love of my life, but the mirror that reflects back the woman I was always destined to become. Before you, I had glimpses of my power. With you, I learned how to live fully in it. You have shown me what unwavering leadership, patience, and unconditional love look like in real time. Through your example, I discovered what it means to be cherished, respected, and challenged to rise higher.

You didn't just teach me how to build businesses; you taught me the *art of people*. You helped me understand human emotion, the beauty of patience, and the power of perseverance. You pour-wisdom into me daily, reminding me that high value isn't just something we talk about, it's something we *become.* You helped me sharpen my voice, shape my vision, and believe that I was capable of more than I ever imagined.

We are more than husband and wife; we are destiny partners. Together, we dream, we build, we expand, and we evolve. You have pulled out of me things I didn't even know were there: the leader, the teacher, the queen. Your faith in me made me stretch beyond comfort and step boldly into purpose. And through your unwavering belief in me, I found the strength to empower other women to do the same.

You also brought clarity to one of the most confusing areas for so many women's relationships. You helped me see the truth: that we often become delusional about what to expect from love because we don't yet know our worth. Your wisdom helped me rise above fantasy and root myself in reality, showing me that healthy love doesn't diminish. And that's the message I hope every woman feels as she reads these pages.

This book is not just my story, it's our story, a formula for women that's tired of mediocrity. It's the story of how alignment attracts destiny, how authenticity builds trust, and how two people can become partners in purpose. I honor and respect you deeply, Kevin for your patience, for your strength, for your leadership, and for the way you love me without conditions. Thank you for creating a space where I can be fully myself unfiltered, unmasked, and unapologetically me.

And because you gave me that gift, I now dedicate my life to helping other women give that same gift to themselves so that they, too, can attract a love that feels like purpose, not pressure.

With every word of this book, I honor God and the man who believed in me before I fully believed in myself.

ABOUT ME: MELISSA PORTIS

Before I became the woman I am today, I didn't know my worth. I lived in fear, fear of what people thought, fear of disappointing my family, fear of disappointing the church. And if I'm being real? I let those fears run my life.

I was taught to dim my light to make others comfortable. If my makeup was too bright, it was "the devil." If I wore pants, I would be "rebellious." If I asked questions, I was "disrespectful." I took on other people's opinions of me so much that I forgot who Melissa even was.

The Bible says, *"Come as you are."* But instead of letting God do His work in me, I let man-made rules tear me down. I thought every setback, every insecurity, every heartbreak was a spiritual attack. In reality, it was me living small, believing lies about myself, ignoring the voice of God that had been guiding me in prophetic dreams since I was a young girl.

I grew up in a loving two parent household where I was celebrated for the small wins, but deep down I felt like I was never "enough." I tried to live up to everyone else's expectations; my parents, the church, society and I lost myself in the process. I was a chronic people pleaser. In relationships, friendships, and even in my career, I abandoned myself to keep the peace.

But there came a point when I had to wake up. Like the moment in scripture in Luke 24 when the disciples' eyes opened as they realized it was Jesus they were breaking bread with. When things started to click, my eyes opened. I saw the world, and myself, clearly. I realized this is God's movie, and I'm simply one of the cast members playing my part boldly and unapologetically. I stopped blaming everything on the devil and started taking responsibility for my power.

I started having deep talks with myself in the mirror, morning and night, soaking in scripture and affirmations until I truly believed it: *Melissa, you are worthy. Melissa, you are powerful. Melissa, you are a bad bit*** in the best way! I stopped dimming my light.

I stepped fully into alignment with who God created me to be.

And everything changed.

Today, I'm a certified nutritionist and transformational coach helping women strengthen their health, mindset, relationships, and overall well-being. I specialize in helping women break free from the "I can't" mentality and empowering them to be the best version of themselves, shifting them from self-sabotage to self-mastery using CBT, REBT, NLP, and neuroscience-backed methods. I'm also certified in emotional intelligence, helping women build resilience, rediscover their identity, and step into their feminine power.

Together with my hubby, my King, my partner, run **SnuggFitt**, our wellness boutique. We do fitness training, create custom nutrition and workout plans, provide life coaching, including a meal prep and catering business tailored to each client's body type and lifestyle. We use advanced bioscan technology to help clients identify deficiencies in their body and create personalized plans to restore balance. Whether online or in person, my mission is simple: help people live healthy, whole, and free.

But my calling goes deeper than fitness and nutrition. I'm here to help women wake up to their worth, step into their confidence, and attract love that they deserve not love that requires them to shrink. Everything I've learned, everything I've overcome, I pour into this work. Because when a woman knows who she is? She becomes unstoppable.

This is my story. This is my purpose. If these words found you, trust that it's not by accident God aligned this moment for you to rise, too!

www.ingramcontent.com/pod-product-compliance
Lightning Source LLC
LaVergne TN
LVHW010618100826
845148LV00014B/3020

* 9 7 9 8 2 1 8 8 2 3 1 2 2 *